# CLOSER READINGS *of the* COMMON CORE

# CLOSER READINGS
## of the COMMON CORE

## Asking Big Questions About the English/Language Arts Standards

**PATRICK SHANNON,** *EDITOR*

HEINEMANN
Portsmouth, NH

Heinemann
361 Hanover Street
Portsmouth, NH 03801–3912
www.heinemann.com

*Offices and agents throughout the world*

*Credits continue on page xvi.*

**Library of Congress Cataloging-in-Publication Data**
Closer readings of the common core : asking big questions about the English/language arts standards / Patrick Shannon, Editor.
     pages cm
  Includes bibliographical references and index.
  ISBN: 978-0-325-04876-5
  1. Language arts—Standards—United States. 2. English language—Study and teaching—Standards—United States. 3. Education—Standards—United States.  I. Shannon, Patrick, 1951– author, editor of compilation.
  LB1576.C5657 2013
  372.6—dc23                                                      2013020665

*Acquisitions editor:* Tobey Antao
*Production:* Patty Adams
*Cover and interior designs:* Lisa A. Fowler and Suzanne Heiser
*Typesetter:* Valerie Levy, Drawing Board Studios
*Manufacturing:* Steve Bernier

Printed in the United States of America on acid-free paper
17   16   15   14   13   VP   1   2   3   4   5

# CONTENTS

# CONTRIBUTORS

**Peggy Albers** is a professor in the College of Education at Georgia State University in Atlanta. She teaches literacy education courses at the graduate level, works with preservice teacher preparation in the field of English education, and also works with inservice teachers in literacy. Her current interests are semiotics, digital and media texts, visual discourse analysis, and children's literature.

**Randy Bomer** is a professor and chair of Curriculum and Instruction at the University of Texas at Austin. A former president of the NCTE, he chaired one of the groups that provided early responses to the CCS—and who knows, they might have been even worse. Randy's books with Heinemann include *Building Adolescent Literacy in Today's English Classroom*, *For a Better World*, and *Time for Meaning*.

**Catherine Compton-Lilly** is an associate professor in Curriculum and Instruction at the University of Wisconsin at Madison. Dr. Compton-Lilly teaches courses in literacy studies and works with professional development schools in Madison. Her interests include examining how time operates as a contextual factor in children's lives as they progress through school and construct their identities as students and readers. Dr. Compton-Lilly is the author/editor of several books and has published widely in educational journals.

**Curt Dudley-Marling** teaches courses in language and literacy in the Lynch School of Education at Boston College. His scholarly interests include the social construction of learning failures, the power of "high expectation" curricula, classroom discussion, and disability studies. His most recent book (with Sarah Michaels) is *The Power of High-Expectation Curricula: Helping All Students Succeed with Powerful Learning* (Teachers College Press).

**Elizabeth Jaeger** is a former elementary teacher. She is currently an assistant professor in the department of Teaching, Learning, and Sociocultural Studies at the University of Arizona.

**Joanne Larson** is the Michael W. Scandling Professor of Education and chair of the Teaching and Curriculum department in the Margaret Warner Graduate School of Education and Human Development at the University of Rochester.

**Marjorie Faulstich Orellana** is a professor of Urban Schooling in the Graduate School of Education and Information Studies at the University of California at Los Angeles and director of faculty for the Teacher Education Program. She was a bilingual classroom teacher in Los Angeles from 1983 to 1993. The author of *Translating Childhoods: Immigrant Youth, Language and Culture*, her research examines the language and literacy practices of youth in urban multilingual communities, and especially the work that the children of immigrants do as language and culture brokers.

**Gloria-Beatriz Rodríguez** is a Ph.D. candidate in Urban Schooling at the Graduate School of Education and Information Studies at the University of California at Los Angeles. A former public school administrator and legal aide attorney, Beatriz conducts research with children and youth exploring the relationship of hip hop cultural practices and modes to learning and language theory and innovative teaching practice. Her focus on hip hop culture's visual element of "stylewriting" (urban calligraphy) aims to disrupt schooling paradigms and build new pathways into our understanding of kids' creative, symbolic, multimodal languaging capacities and potentials.

A former preschool and primary grade teacher, **Patrick Shannon** teaches courses and directs the Summer Reading Camp in the reading specialist program at Pennsylvania State University. Most recently, he is the author of *Reading Wide Awake* (Teachers College) and *Reading Poverty in America* (Routledge).

**Kristopher Stewart** is currently a doctoral student in literacy studies at the University of Wisconsin at Madison. His research interests include literacy and identity, the sociocultural contexts of literacy, academic language and literacy, and family and community literacy practices. He can be reached at stewart3@wisc.edu.

**Sandra Wilde** is the author of several books about literacy including, most recently, *Funner Grammar*. She lives in New York City, where she teaches at Hunter College and works with teachers and children at P.S./I.S. 180 in Harlem.

**Maja Wilson** teaches literacy courses at the University of Maine. She won the James A. Britton Award from the Conference on English Education, NCTE for *Rethinking Rubrics in Writing Assessment* (Heinemann).

# FOREWORD

## *Operationalizing the Neoliberal Common Good*
### » JOANNE LARSON

Developed by the National Governors Association Center for Best Practices (NGA Center) and the Council of Chief State School Officers (CCSSO), the Common Core State Standards (CCSS) are an attempt to establish a national set of unified educational goals and outcomes that follows the neoliberal agenda to standardize education. A key feature of the neoliberal agenda is government through the market, wherein education is viewed as a consumer-driven commodity that ought to be efficient and profitable (e.g., privatized) (deAlba, Gonzales-Gaudiano, Lankshear, and Peters 2000). Standardization, in this view, works toward efficiency and competition for market share. What emerges as a purpose of schooling in this model is the production of an efficient and marketable worker, a key component of the CCSS emphasis on college and career.

Traditional purposes of schooling have always emphasized that schools should prepare youth for work and/or for citizenship. Variously and according to political whims of the time, one or the other of these purposes takes precedence in public discourse, though it is unclear the extent to which any aim has actually been accomplished. A classic example of a swing in emphasis between worker/citizen purpose was the U.S. reaction to the launch of Sputnik in 1957. With Sputnik, we experienced a rabid return to so-called "basics" followed by calls for winning the space race through U.S. innovations in science and math. New curricula were designed and implemented, which failed miserably. Social movements of the 1960s saw a shift back to meaning and citizenship as purposes of schooling; however, the 1983 release of *A Nation At Risk* with its fear-based calls for economic competition (we were losing the race again) snapped us back to the "basics" with which we are currently faced. Goals 2000, No Child Left Behind (NCLB), Race To The Top (RTTT), and now the CCSS are all extensions of this basic skills backlash. The CCSS continuation of the back-to-basics backlash appears to preclude the citizenship purpose altogether in its exclusive focus on preparation for college and career. None of these changes in emphasis between worker in a globally competitive marketplace or citizen in a democracy has resulted in a just and equitable education system (Larson, forthcoming). Furthermore, all of the historical purposes of schooling are outmoded given changes in Internet and communication technologies and the changed and changing literacy practices therein.

Building on traditional, outmoded purposes of schooling where schools are positioned as either training workers or building citizens, the CCSS argue that in order to compete in a global marketplace and to prepare students for college and careers (worker purpose), the nation needs a consistent set of national benchmarks so that "we the people" can know students will be adequately prepared no matter where they live (Common Core State Standards 2012). Yet the standards position the population to be competitive in a global marketplace without articulating what that global marketplace is or what being competitive therein means. *Adequately prepared* is also not defined, nor is the *what* for which they are to be prepared. Knowing where we are going and, more importantly, why we are going there is key to authentic change.

Moreover, the CCSS imply a common good that is not defined or at least assumes a kind of "norm" that does not exist in the United States. However, given our history with standardization, we can assume that the "common" means this mythical American "norm" that is centered on white, middle-class values and practices. Furthermore, we can see the economic emphasis of the CCSS goals that may also be assumed to be a "common" good:

> The Common Core State Standards provide a consistent, clear understanding of what students are expected to learn, so teachers and parents know what they need to do to help them. The standards are designed to be robust and relevant to the real world,

reflecting the knowledge and skills that our young people need for *success in college and careers*. With American students fully prepared for the future, our communities will be best positioned *to compete successfully in the global economy*. (Common Core Standards State 2012, emphasis added)

Economic purposes of schooling take precedence in these standards as evidenced by the goal to position students as competitive in a global economy, again reflecting the market focus of the neoliberal agenda. We can see the hegemony of historical purposes, such as the preparation of workers, as they resurface in contemporary "standards"—however, the "citizen" purpose seems to be missing. State departments of education require these standards in order for schools to maintain their funding. College and career readiness is a central feature of the RTTT federal funding policy, for example, and states have to indicate how they will meet this goal in order to keep their funding. Is this a common good? Who should decide what counts as the common good? Along with the authors in this volume, I am not sure we want the authors of the CCSS to establish that good, especially if it means a return to narrow definitions of what constitutes literacy.

Upon closer examination, it seems apparent that the primary beneficiaries of this "common" good are companies like the Gates Foundation and Pearson as well as other corporations who will supply materials for adoption and implementation. For example, Gates is funding a series of curriculum mappings (www.commoncore.org/maps/) aligned with the Common Core and Pearson will publish the tests (http://commoncore.pearsoned.com). Alignment to the test is a key function of the Gates curriculum mappings.

The CCSS have a singular, normative focus on an outmoded purpose of schooling as preparation for participation in a global economy via traditional college and career pathways. The trajectory is normative in that it is expected that everyone follow the same path; however, details about that path are not outlined. As Foucault (1979) argues, normalization is a key technique of disciplinary power that is implemented in schools, prisons, and other public institutions. Nonconformity is punished in a variety of ways (bad grades, suspensions, reprimands) that compare, differentiate, hierarchize, homogenize, and exclude. It is these punishment strategies that construct and maintain the norm, and that will be a part of the institutionalization of the CCSS and their aligned tests.

We know that a person has achieved this normative goal when she/he has scored above average on a standardized test. Standardization as sameness is the key here (Gutiérrez 2007). This sameness is required in spite of the incredible diversity of human life. In this traditional view, schooling focuses on getting everyone to the central goal that is based on "normed" practices stemming from the early days of U.S. schooling when the idea was to assimilate students into a uniform citizenry and to weed out the rubbish (Jefferson [1784] 1954). We can argue about what that norm is, but many have shown that what it ends up being is for us all to conform to white, middle-class interaction and academic norms (Heath 1983; hooks 1994). The developmental trajectory for all students is unidirectional (toward the norm) and success is measured on standardized metrics that hold the norm constant.

Another consequence of normed standardization may be that the social contract of school is irrevocably broken by these hegemonic instrumentalist discourses that privilege the rational subject (Biesta 2009). By social contract I mean the mutual understanding that "we the people" trust that schools will educate our children and youth well and that schools will do no harm. However, NCLB (U.S. Department of Education 2012a), RTTT (U.S. Department of Education 2012b), and now the CCSS undermine that contract by reinforcing flawed assumptions about knowledge production and learning underlying the current U.S. system (Larson, forthcoming). The current high-stakes testing environment does damage children (Nichols & Berliner 2007). Just because it is the law does not make it right; many, many laws have been just plain wrong. The emphasis on achievement and achievement scores, and new laws that link student test scores to teacher evaluation in spite of the lack of evidence explaining the connection, are just plain wrong. National level standardization such as that being proposed by the CCSS is also just wrong in a complex, pluralistic society, or at least going in the wrong direction.

I want to be clear that I am not arguing that children and youth should not have equal access to college and the careers of their choosing, rather just the opposite—all children and youth have a right to equal access to these discourses of power (Morrell 2008). I am arguing that global competitiveness articulated through the neoliberal agenda, as a purpose of education, is wrongheaded and will not result in either a just and equitable education system or in readiness for college and career. Furthermore, I argue that the predominant discourses of power about achievement and global competition need to change in order for us to begin to achieve justice and equity, certainly a worthy purpose of education (Larson forthcoming). Our focus needs to be on human well-being, meaning making, and knowledge production—not on producing efficient, compliant workers and noncritical citizens (Biesta 2011).

Authors in this volume take seriously the challenge of analyzing the CCSS for both their advantages and disadvantages. All are concerned with issues of equity and justice in their discussions. Authors present what positives the CCSS offer (such as the belief that all children are capable of complex learning) and also critique the standards for what, and who, they leave out. Overall, the CCSS was complimented for their emphasis on close reading of texts in ways that may accomplish higher-order thinking. However, authors overwhelmingly question the need for such standards and pointedly ask whose standards are represented and whose are left out. There are several points they make that are worth noting here.

- The CCSS narrow the practices and identities available to children, positioning every child as a future college student—eliminating choice and desire in the process.
- The CCSS assume knowledge is static and exists outside of human meaning making; standards are the same across levels, but are "simpler" at younger grades. This sequencing assumes knowledge can be broken into bits, made simpler, and sequenced according to developmental stage—something sociocultural theory has successfully challenged.
- A singular "common core" does not account for the diversity of social and cultural practices children bring to schools, and authors worry that the Common Core will exacerbate current inequities. They argue that high standards as minimum requirements do not address the achievement gap nor will they ameliorate the effects of poverty.

- Given our history with standards and testing, there is nothing in the "new standards and new tests" argument that will change the neoliberal emphasis on market-based consumerism grounded in competition, choice, and hyperaccountability that remains at the forefront of educational reform.
- The CCSS emphasize that meaning is in the text, not in the interaction between reader and text. This separation positions readers as subservient to text and divorces them from personal engagement. This point is echoed in several chapters through discussions about how the CCSS may exacerbate current inequities since children's funds of knowledge are not accounted for in standardization. Furthermore, text is narrowly defined as the written word in ways that exclude complex texts that are apparent in contemporary times (e.g., tweets, video, blogs, etc.).
- Teachers are positioned as not knowing how to develop curriculum, which puts them in the role of consumer of prepackaged modules marketed by textbook companies. Furthermore, professional development is defined as a bureaucratic process and an economic decision. We know from years of research on high-quality professional development that, at minimum, teachers need to be in charge of their own professional development.

In the end and as these authors point out, the CCSS are based on an autonomous definition of literacy that does not account for ideological definitions that position literacy as social practices that are radically context specific and always imbued in relations of power. As a result, the CCSS will not result in college-ready students who will go gently into the workforce.

# REFERENCES

Biesta, G. 2009. "Education and the Democratic Person: Towards a Political Conception of Democratic Education." *Teachers College Record* 109 (3): 740–69.

———. 2011. "The Ignorant Citizen: Mouffe, Ranciere, and the Subject of Democratic Education." *Studies in the Philosophy of Education* 30: 141–53.

Common Core Standards. 2012. Accessed February 12. http://www.corestandards.org/.

deAlba, A., E. Gonzalez-Gaudino, C. Lankshear, and M. Peters. 2000. *Curriculum in the Postmodern Condition.* New York: Lang.

Foucault, M. 1979. *Discipline and Punish: The Birth of the Prison.* Translated by A. Sheridan. New York: Random House.

Gutiérrez, K. 2007. "'Sameness as Fairness': The New Tonic of Equality and Opportunity." In *Literacy as Snake Oil: Beyond the Quick Fix*, edited by J. Larson, 109–22. New York: Lang.

Heath, S. B. 1982. "What No Bedtime Story Means: Narrative Skills at Home and School." *Language in Society*: 49–76.

hooks, b. 1994. *Teaching to Transgress: Education as the Practice of Freedom.* New York: Routledge.

Jefferson, T. (1784) 1954. *The Founders' Constitution, Volume 1, Chapter 18, Document 16.* Chicago: University of Chicago Press. Accessed August 6, 2012. http://press-pubs.uchicago.edu/founders/documents/v1ch18s16.html.

Larson, J. forthcoming. *Radical Equality and Education: Starting Over in American Schooling.* New York: Routledge.

Morrell, E. 2008. *Critical Literacy and Urban Youth: Pedagogies of Access, Dissent, and Liberation.* New York: Routledge.

Nichols, S., and D. Berliner. 2007. *Collateral Damage: How High-Stakes Testing Corrupts America's Schools.* Cambridge, MA: Harvard Education Press.

U.S. Department of Education. 2012a. Accessed January 15. http://www2.ed.gov/nclb/landing.jhtml?src=ln.

U.S. Department of Education. 2012b. Accessed January 15. http://www2.ed.gov/programs/racetothetop/index.html.

# CHAPTER 1

## An Evidence Base for the Common Core

>> PATRICK SHANNON

*How'd we get here?*

During the 2010 National Governors Association meeting in Washington, DC, President Obama offered the rationale for the official Common Core Standards (CCS):

> [Asian nations] want their kids to excel because they understand that whichever country out-educates the other is going to out-compete us in the future. So that's what we're up against. That's what's at stake—nothing less than our primacy in the world. . . . And I want to commend all of you for acting collectively through the National Governors Association to develop common academic standards that will better position our students for success.

And at the 2009 National Conference of State Legislatures in Philadephia, Bill Gates explained how the standards would do their work:

> Identifying common standards is just the starting point. We'll only know if this effort has succeeded when the curriculum and the tests are aligned to these standards. Secretary of Education Arne Duncan recently announced that $350 million of the stimulus package will be used to create just these kinds of tests—next

generation assessments aligned with the common core. When the tests are aligned with the common standards, the curriculum will line up as well, and it will unleash a powerful market of people providing services for better teaching. For the first time, there will be a large uniform base of customers looking at using products that can help every kid learn and every teacher get better.

In these two statements, the two most powerful voices on American education present the promise and the peril of CCS. They show that state officials want our kids to excel for personal success and U.S. leadership in the world. The CCS demonstrate that we are forward thinking people, with shared core values, who are capable of working our way out of the Great Recession in order to face continuous global economic challenges. The promise of America, then, is to be found in the enhanced education of our citizens. Sign me up!

Yet the president and Mr. Gates are national figures cajoling state officials about public education—a state's right. In order to explain their interpretation of America's apparent decline, both assume that schools lack standards and that teachers don't teach well. Moreover, the president implies ("common academic standards that will better position"), and Gates explains directly ("we'll only know if this effort has succeeded"), the mechanism for enhancing education is to be found in the tight alignment from standards to learning through national testing and national markets for teaching tools. In my father's terms, "they put their money where their mouth is," offering cash-strapped states and districts financial incentives to accept "the solution." This suggests, at least to me, that our collectivity and shared core might be more economic, and less altruistic, in character. Might I borrow an eraser?

In this chapter, I take up the context of the CCS, discussing their history, rationale, and development in order to provide some understanding of how three powerful discourses represented in President Obama's and Bill Gates' statements swirl around and through the lives of teachers and students. After a brief review of the Common Core lineage, I examine the scientific evidentiary base for the rationale, the role of business within their development, and the federal government's involvement in their implementation. Rather than the closed rational representation presented in the quotations above, I see CCS as a value-laden, open project in continuous development—just waiting for teachers, parents, and students to step forward in order to negotiate their design as well as their enactment in classrooms.

## CCS HISTORY

Advocates connect the CCS with over sixty years of sincere efforts to improve the performance of public schools. For example, the Council on Foreign Relations (Klein and Rice 2012) recommend the CCS in order to prepare citizens to serve and protect the United States' interests around the world in a manner reminiscent of the National Defense Act of 1958—to lead the world in math, science, and foreign language. Linda Darling Hammond (2010) understands a carefully implemented Common Core as a lynchpin in a more equitable distribution of school benefits across social class (Elementary and Secondary Education Act of 1965), race (*Brown v. Board of Education* 1954), and (dis)ability (Education for All Handicapped Children Act of 1975). Through its Developing Futures in Education initiative, the GE Foundation (2012) funds the implementation of CCS in seven cities and exhorts business leaders to promote the standards as the means to increase citizens' economic productivity and competitiveness (Smith Hughes Act of 1917, Servicemen Readjustment Act of 1944, No Child Left Behind 2002). In these ways, CCS are intended to further historic missions of national security, equal opportunity, and human capital development.

In a slightly different light, CCS can be seen as a culmination of thirty years of direct calls to increase the academic rigor of failing American schools. The *A Nation at Risk* report (National Commission on Excellence in Education 1983) told us, "If an unfriendly foreign power had attempted to impose on America the mediocre educational performance that exists today, we might well have viewed it as an act of war" (7). Accordingly, state officials were to raise graduation requirements for all students, develop more robust curricula within all disciplines, and improve their teaching core through better training and higher salaries. Standing before members of the National Governors

Association, philanthropic organizations, and large corporations in 1991, President Bush announced the America 2000 education policy initiative, which challenged schools to graduate 90 percent of their students after they demonstrated competence in challenging subject matter at the end of primary grades, middle school, and high school. A clear champion of these actions at the time, Diane Ravitch (1995) explained, "These goals implied the need for some kind of national standards and national testing" (58).

In 1992, the Department of Education awarded the International Reading Association (IRA), the National Council of Teachers of English (NCTE), and the Center for the Study of Reading a $3 million grant to develop just such standards for English language arts. Eighteen months into the project, however, government officials terminated it for lack of "substantial progress." The IRA and NCTE eventually published their version of English language arts standards (www.ncte.org/standards/ncte-ira)—a twelve-statement document that did not include the "specification of content—what students should know and be able to do" that the federal government sought (National Council of Education Standards and Testing 1992, 3). Direct federal involvement in the development of national academic standards ended with Congress' vote to condemn the national history standards in 1994. In President Clinton's proposal for, and then President Bush's version of the reauthorization of the Elementary and Secondary Education Act, states were required to produce rigorous standards and examinations (and submit them to the federal government for approval) in order to verify each student's adequate yearly progress toward proficiency in English language arts and math.

At the 1996 Education Summit, representatives of the National Governors Association, philanthropic foundations, and business established Achieve to broker support for rigorous state academic standards. Funded generously by the Battelle, Gates, Cisco, GE, JP Morgan, and Hewitt foundations and the Boeing, IBM, Lumina, and State Farm corporations (http://www.achieve.org/contributors), Achieve's effectiveness can be demonstrated through its Academic Standards and Assessment Benchmarking Pilot Project and the American Diploma Project that culminated in the *Ready or Not: Creating a High School Diploma That Counts* report in 2004. In that report, Achieve identified what it labeled the "common core of English and mathematics academic knowledge or skills (or benchmarks) that

American high school students need for success in college and the workforce" (www.achieve.org/history-achieve). In its subsequent work, Achieve established an annual review of states' progress toward developing grade level standards leading to that Common Core (*Closing the Expectations Gap* 2006–2012). In 2008, Achieve discovered "a remarkable degree of consistency in English and mathematics requirements" among states for high school graduation (*Out of Many, One* 2008). In 2009, Achieve partnered with the National Governors Association and the Council of Chief State School Officers in the formal production of the CCS at each grade level, serving as the project manager as well. In 2010, Achieve became the project manager for Partnership for Assessment of Readiness for College and Careers (PARCC), one of the two organizations federally funded to produce Common Core assessments by 2014. In 2011, Achieve began work on Next Generation (K–12) Science Standards.

The final versions of CCS for English language arts and mathematics were produced within twelve months (June 2009 to June 2, 2010). According to its blue ribbon Validation Committee (2010), the CCS process exceeded the principles the National Governors Association Center for Best Practices and the Council of Chief State School Officers set for standards development. Members of a writing team negotiated drafts with a separate working group of English language arts experts, circulating drafts through state departments of education and one public review. According to the Common Core website, the writers fielded over ten thousand comments. In its final report, the Validation Committee concluded, "Unlike past standards-setting efforts, the Common Core State Standards are based on best practices in national and international education, as well as research and input from numerous sources" (p. 4). Although not formally credited in the CCS documents, David Coleman, a member of the English Language Arts Work Team, is acknowledged as the "quiet" architect of those standards (Hess 2012; Ravitch 2012; Rotherham 2011; Toppo 2012). (Coleman's [2011a] demonstrations of curricular choices and lesson design are instructive in understanding the developers' expectations for implementation in classrooms.)

Throughout the development process and into current implementation efforts, CCS officials have insisted that the federal government "had no role in the development of the common core state standards and will not have a role in their implementation." Yet from the beginning, two states (Texas and Alaska) declined to participate because their governors feared a loss of state control over educational matters. Currently, four states (add Minnesota and Virginia) have yet to adopt the CCS as the model for their state standards. These and other concerned parties point to four federal moves "intended" to compel states to adopt the CCS.

1) In the same speech to the National Governors Association quoted at the beginning of this chapter, President Obama announced that he would like to make federal Title 1 funding contingent on states adopting the CCS (Klein 2010).

2) In RTTT regulations, states that adopted the CCS by August 2, 2010, were awarded extra points in the competition for a portion of $4.5 billion in federal funding (Lewin 2010).

3) In exchange for agreeing to adopt the CCS and other favored policies, Secretary of Education Arne Duncan granted states waivers from adequate yearly progress quotas set under the NCLB law, saving many schools from being categorized as "failing" (Perez-Pena 2012).

4) As Bill Gates mentioned in the quote cited at the beginning of this chapter, the federal government provided $350 million to two agencies (Smarter Balanced Assessment Consortium [SBAC] and PARCC) to develop Common Core assessments.

Critics argue that each of these incentives made (and make) it difficult for state officials to "choose" not to adopt the CCS. In their eyes, these acts turn CCS into de facto national standards—an illegality under the original ESEA statute, if mandated by federal authorities.

Creating another concern about "national standards, curriculum and assessment," David Coleman became the president of the College Board in the fall of 2012 with the expressed intention to base the SAT and Advanced Placement curricula and tests on the CCS. This is precisely part of Gates' steps for aligning schooling around the CCS. Although the PARCC and SBAC assessments in all subjects could eventually render the SAT moot,

Common Core curricula for all Advanced Placement courses and evaluations would add academic leverage to the federal and philanthropic financial incentives, inveigling states to adopt and maintain the Common Core against their better judgments.

The ongoing nature of history is a challenge to anyone attempting to provide context for an event or artifact—history just keeps happening, and as more people consider that context, they find new connections in the past as well. At this moment (the fall of 2012), the CCS straddle the tensions within schooling for economic development, equality of opportunity, and global standing. Advocates explain that CCS will meliorate the tensions, and they work strategically to complete the positioning of students for success (Obama) by aligning standards with curricula and assessments (Gates). They worry because, although forty-six states have adopted CCS at this point, there are no guarantees that officials from even these states will produce or purchase common curricula, adopt common assessments, or set common passing scores. Despite rhetoric to the contrary, the standards are still open to interpretation, and the alignment project is still being negotiated. These are wide-open spaces for teachers, students, and community members to step into in order to participate in the decisions that affect public education.

## EVIDENCE FOR CCS RATIONALES

In their statements, President Obama and Bill Gates provide two connected rationales for CCS. First and foremost, they argue that the United States is falling behind other countries in the new global innovation economy, and it's because our education system is failing. Second, they locate the remedy for that situation in the realignment of the education system according to a single set of world-class standards that will improve individual and national performance, productivity, and competitiveness. Even governors critical of the "federal" CCSS seem to accept these two rationales as evidence-based and accurate (e.g., Mark Dayton, Nikki Haley, and Rick Perry). Yet others examine that same evidence and ask questions about whether it offers a sufficient basis for the great expense of standards production and school alignment.

## Is America Falling Behind Economically?

These are decidedly hard economic times for many in the United States. However, few can point with justification toward schools as the cause of these hardships or as the immediate remedy for our sluggish economy. And things aren't too much better elsewhere. In international comparisons, Americans enjoy (perhaps not equally) the world's largest economy—still twice as large as its nearest competitor, China. Goldin and Katz (2008) give schools partial credit for the expansion of the U.S. economy during the first half of the twentieth century, but offer no credit to schools for the continuation of America's economic growth during the second half or into the twenty-first century.

We must face facts, though. Eventually, China will catch the United States economically—not because the United States is declining, but because China's workforce is four times larger. Currently, Chinese workers need only be 1/4 as productive as their American counterparts in order to maintain its relative status. Any increase in Chinese productivity, and their economy gains ground regardless of American productivity. Since the 1950s, American workers' productivity has increased steadily, accelerating rather sharply after 1995. Former secretary of labor Robert Reich (2011) attributes the increase to the rise of technology in the workplace (often displacing workers) and explains that many other countries have relatively the same access to such technology as the United States. Eventually, he reports that America's twentieth-century economic advantages will vanish in a competitive world.

## Is Education Responsible for Worker Productivity?

Economist Ha-Joon Chang (2010) doesn't think so: "What really matters in the determination of national prosperity is not the educational level of individuals, but the nation's ability to organize individuals into enterprises with high productivity" (179). The ability to organize productively relies on governments' capacity to provide a range of institutions that encourage investment and risk-taking—a trade regime that protects infant industries; a financial system that provides for patent capitalization; good bankruptcy laws to protect capitalists and a good social safety net to support workers in times of trouble; and public subsidies and regulation for research, development, and training. These are the changes that led to the economic success in the Asian countries that President Obama mentioned. During the last half century, each has realigned its government in order to provide these institutions and policies. Their education systems are a consequence, not the cause, of this realignment and rise. Truth be told, the American government facilitated many of these international changes and provided incentives for American business to participate in the expansions at the expense of American labor (Reich 2011).

Certainly, global economic policy is beyond the reach of American education. Although many from all political stripes argue that the design of American schools was (is) organized to teach workers appropriate dispositions (Bowles and Gintus 1976; Callahan 1962; Hess 2010; Ravitch 2010), most school subjects were (are) never intended to raise worker productivity directly—I'm thinking of the arts, literature, and history. Does that limit their value? Some think so. For example, both Obama and Gates call for more attention to math, science, and technology, and the CCS increase the informational text load for students at every grade in order to ready workers for careers or college (then careers). But even those work "related" academic subjects do not have strong associations with economic development (Wolf 2002), and we can see that in the very test scores to which Obama and Gates point (Loveless 2012).

Consider the international rankings among countries according to reading and math scores. On the 2009 Program for International Student Assessment (PISA) for reading, American students were listed seventeenth among nations—behind the Asian nations as President Obama mentioned, but also behind Poland, Iceland, and Estonia. In math, American students were slotted thirty-first—behind Slovenia, the United Kingdom, and Portugal. It's difficult to imagine an economic rubric that would rank all these economies higher than ours. Chang (2010) reports that the amount and quality of schooling is not even highly correlated with worker productivity—let alone causally linked. Does that mean that we should deemphasize traditional school subjects? Not if we believe those subjects will enrich students' lives and help them to become good citizens.

## Does the Global Innovation Economy Require
## Workers to Acquire New Skills?

Remember the knowledge economy is not new. Command over knowledge has always provided economic advantage through technologies. Think China in the first century with paper, movable type, gunpowder, and the compass; Britain in the nineteenth; or the United States in the first half of the twentieth century. These advantaged positions, however, do not mean that every worker in those circumstances commanded that valued knowledge or enjoyed its benefits equally. Thomas Friedman (2012) makes this point indirectly, but clearly. He calls for the U.S. Congress to abandon its efforts to bring Internet access to rural America, diverting those resources in order to provide "ultra high speed bandwidth to the top 5 percent in university towns, which invent the future." The smart cities around universities, he tells us, must have "an educated populace" with "abundant human intellectual capital" who will "engage in high performance knowledge exchanges," using "intelligent objects" to mine data, analyze it, and discover new goods and services. The remaining 95 percent, he continues, must learn to accommodate the flows of resources into smart cities and to support the distribution of the innovations out from their borders. Friedman claims this is America's only hope to preserve its middle class.

In this way, the combination of employing technology to improve productivity and the redeployment of resources to support the innovative 5 percent does not translate into new skill demands or the need for more education among the 95 percent who are to service this economy. (Of course, that's only true if we continue to buy the rationale that the primary purpose of schooling is to make all students career or college ready.) The U.S. Bureau of Labor Statistics (2012) represents this reality in its estimate of the thirty fastest growing jobs between 2010 and 2020. Twenty-one of the jobs require a high school diploma, perhaps (e.g., a variety of health aides, construction laborers of many types, and bicycle repair[?]); six require a BA (health educator, marriage therapist, and event planner); and only three require professional training (veterinarian, biomedical engineer, and physical therapist). All of these occupations and many of the ones that are not growing as fast could require new dispositions, perhaps in order to manage more independence from direct supervision, but they don't seem to require new academic knowledge and skills as claimed in the rationales for CCS. And if it's new independent dispositions that we need, then will an aligned forced system of education help us to develop them?

## Are American Schools Failing?

During the Reagan administration, the *A Nation at Risk* report claimed that students were not reaching the same levels of literacy as their parents and grandparents, and therefore school reform was urgently needed. In a government-sponsored report, the Sandia Laboratory proved the claim to be false—student test scores in the 1980s were higher than during the 1960s or 1940s. Although President George H. W. Bush never released the report, the findings were circulated and published in *The Manufactured Crisis* (Berliner and Biddle 1995). And at least some scores are still rising. For nine-year-olds, National Assessment of Educational Progress (NAEP) scores were twelve points higher between 1978 and 2008—though for seventeen-year-olds the scores remained about the same (Drum 2012). Not overwhelmingly successful, but certainly not failing.

Comparisons of international reading scores (Berliner 2009; Bracey 2009; Krashen, Lee, and McQuillan 2010) demonstrate that there are two American public school systems—one for the middle class and one for the poor. American schools with few students eligible for free or reduced-cost lunches score at or above the top international scores, and schools with high concentrations of eligible students place among the lowest scoring nations. This achievement gap between rich and poor school systems has increased by 40 percent since 1970 (Reardon 2011) as income segregation within metropolitan areas has doubled (Reardon and Bischoff 2011) and the incomes of 80 percent of American families have stagnated (U.S. Census Bureau/the *New York Times* 2012). Although these findings make it clear that American public schools do not serve all citizens well, these researchers do not conclude that the public school system is a failure. Rather they identify out-of-school factors and inadequate social policies, as well as in-school factors, that explain the gap between the two systems. They call for coordinated strategies—reminiscent of the War on Poverty—to address poverty, segregation, and school achievement simultaneously.

## Are Common Standards a Key to Closing the Differences Among These Scores?

In the *Brown Center Report on American Education*, Tom Loveless (2012) reminds us that countries scoring above and below the United States on international tests employ national standards, and therefore common standards cannot be the sole cause of high achievement. Although Gates could be correct and common standards aligned with curricula and testing explain high scores, Finland's scores and system confound that conclusion. Finnish schools "produce" high scores, but deemphasize standardized testing (Sahlberg 2011). Like all factors, standards appear to be woven into a network that explains (or doesn't) a country's academic performance. Pulling one strand, like CCS, as the cause of success or failure, is arbitrary at best and misleading at worst. Why not choose the social safety net for families as "the factor"? After all, 80 percent of students in Singapore qualify for and live in public housing, and their scores are higher than ours.

Note also that the income achievement gap persists in every state in the union. This remains true despite the NCLB requirement that each state develop and enact rigorous academic standards. Early in the NCLB process, the Bush administration checked and proclaimed each state to have rigorous standards. If uniformity of standards (a Common Core) were a solution, then the gap *within* states should have narrowed markedly over the last decade. According to Reardon (2011), the racial achievement gap has narrowed slightly; however, the income achievement gap widened during that period. Neither standards nor commonality seem to be key.

## Are Standards Likely to Raise Student Achievement Overall?

The second rationale for CCS assumes that the quality of the standards and the rigor with which they are applied will raise every student's achievement and reduce the gaps that exist among social groups. Building on Whitehurst's (2009) earlier study of the impact of state standards on NAEP scores, however, Loveless (2012) doubts the likely impact of CCS on student achievement beyond what state standards have already achieved. He shows that the quality of the state standards as judged by experts does not predict student achievement; that the rigor of setting high cutoff scores to demonstrate proficiency does not predict student achievement; and that a combination of the two does not predict the narrowing of gaps. Loveless explains, "*Within* state variation is four or five times larger than the variation *between* states" (4, emphasis added). He adopts a popular CCS metaphor to explain this statistical finding. While advocates claim that CCS will overcome the achievement differences *between* Massachusetts and Mississippi students, Loveless shows that every state already has mini-Massachusetts and mini-Mississippi contrasts *within* its borders.

### Are the CCS Rationales Evidence Based?

No—at least not as President Obama and Bill Gates have articulated them, although the English language arts standards themselves could be evidence based. The United States is not behind economically, although all citizens do not share in its success equally. The "new" global innovation economy does not demand new skills for all or even most workers. American schools are not failing generally, although American policies and institutions do not and have not historically served all social groups well. Standards are not easily discernable as a key to difference in academic outcomes among nations or states. And the quality of standards and rigor of alignment are not likely to have the desired effects. In summary, we lack a compelling evidentiary base for the idea of CCS or the subsequent national alignment of curriculum and assessment.

### Why, Then, Did the National Governors Association, the Council of Chief State School Officers, and Four Administrations Spend So Much Time, Energy, and Money to Create the CCS?

And why do so many philanthropic foundations, think tanks, and business groups push them and fund them? Larry Cuban suggests that answers to such questions can be found in the pragmatics of policy making (see http://larrycuban.wordpress.com). Policy makers focus on solving problems, but they don't have ready solutions to apply (or it wouldn't be considered a problem). To begin, policy makers and their associates (this can be a large group—from citizens to support staff to lobbyists of all stripes) struggle to name the problem and to propose possible solutions. Before policy makers try any, they compare and contrast these alternatives in terms of probable costs and benefits until they decide on which one(s) to test in the real world. As Cuban (2010) states, "a policy is both a hypothesis and argument that a particular action should be taken to solve a problem. That action, however, has to be politically acceptable and economically feasible." Although policy making might appear to be a rational process, policy makers must work within established political priorities.

## CCS AS POLITICALLY ACCEPTABLE AND ECONOMICALLY FEASIBLE POLICY

Stripped of their claims of a declining economy, failing schools, and an apparent solution, all that's left in President Obama's and Bill Gates' statements is the development of a national market for technological tools in order to reorganize teaching and learning: "When the tests are aligned with the common standards, the curriculum will line up as well, and it will unleash a powerful market of people providing services for better teaching. For the first time, there will be a large uniform base of customers looking at using products that can help every kid learn and every teacher get better" (Gates 2009). This is a remarkably candid statement that lets political ideology shine through the representation of CCS as a rational solution and their framing of CCS as the means to develop America's human capital in order to compete in the global innovation economy.

An ideology is a shared set of ideas and beliefs that serve to justify and support the interests of a particular group. Gates tells us that national alignment will serve as the catalyst for "a powerful market of people providing services for better teaching" that will invent the future of education. Within this change, schools and teachers become "customers looking at using products" once these innovators complete their designs. It doesn't take a linguist to recognize the relative power of the agents in Gates' hypothesis and argument for CCS. In fact, Gates offers a smaller scale of Friedman's proposal. Public resources currently devoted to public education should be (are being) redirected to private businesses ready to discover new technologies for schools, teachers, and (then) students to consume. In this way, Gates engages in the ideological practice of naming positions for participants through his articulation of apparently normal everyday activities— production and consumption of commodities. And with these positions come expected dispositions—encoded in the standards and modeled in the official demonstrations of CCS practices.

Gates assigns government officials positions as well. Previously ("for the first time"), government regulation of public education as a state right prevented these innovators from producing the needed technologies because the markets were too small and varied. Now, however, with federal backing and state "choice," CCS erases state lines and empowers business to invest and take risks while anticipating sizeable profits through economies of scale. This position fits well with Chang's (2010) explanation of how government action can actually increase a nation's prosperity by organizing actors into productive enterprises. With Gates' phrase and his recommended actions, 150 years of normal governmental practice surrounding public education becomes the barrier in the way of this powerful market and profits.

That's the political ideology of neoliberalism seeping through. Neoliberals pursue traditional liberal goals—individual liberty, equality before the law, and protection of property—using market relations rather than government policies, uniting business, philanthropy, think tanks, government officials, educational experts, taxpayers, school officials, teachers, and students through market solutions. All the key concepts of neoliberalism are included: rule of the market, deregulation, privatization, reduction of public expenditures, and individualism. According to this ideology, by opening public education to market forces, competition among private companies will replace current teaching practices with the most efficient and effective technologies available in a never-ending cycle of creative destruction. This is what "powerful" means in Gates' remarks. In search of profits, businesses ("people providing services for better teaching") will continuously compete to find new ways to meet market demand. If left free from government regulation, these market efficiencies will reduce the labor costs of public education while they improve its effective services to all those individuals who choose to use it as the means to acquire credentials in order to raise personal income potential.

Through this ideological lens, then, the primary problem to be addressed is not how to equalize the two public school systems that serve the better-off and poor, but rather how to create, maintain, and nurture market forces in American public schools (as well as all other aspects of life). CCS and alignment are the hypothesis and the argument to address that problem. In this light, the thirty years of calls for "school reform" from *A Nation at Risk* to RTTT can be understood simply as ideological practices to make the creation of this market and these positions appear normal to the general public and all the participants (despite the history of state and local control). And it seems to have been successful; think about the last time you heard someone or some group with power speak against the neoliberal mantra that American schools are in dire need of reform if we are to compete in the global innovation economy.

Although this market will bring jobs and innovation, the market is not a good set of organizing principles for public education—that is, if you seek policy and action to rectify the existing inequalities. Demand in the market around CCS will create private jobs (and profits) in the design and marketing of new teaching tools (including the tests, of course); at a different income level, it will spawn employment in their manufacture, delivery, and maintenance as well. Each state will need workers to facilitate and to monitor teachers' and students' access to and use of these new technologies, with national companies vying to prepare both groups for measured success. And if the specific demand appears lucrative enough, then niche markets will emerge to provide new tools to address the income and other achievement gaps. In these ways, CCS can have a direct, but not a dramatic, effect on the American economy—although more school funding will likely flow out of or bypass local economies.

Markets are good at distributing resources efficiently to the producers of commodities for which there is the most demand. Producers seek profits and competitive advantage to secure those profits, and consumers seek use and status through their purchase. Self-regulating exchange is a dispassionate individual cash transaction without regard for history, tradition, externalities (location or consequences for people beyond the exchange), or need. The competition among producers pushes continuous innovation for advantage and cost controls to ensure profits within the limits of what consumers are willing (not necessarily able) to pay. Within markets, however, there is little security or stability for the producer, the consumer, or the workers and communities in between them. Innovation can render commodities, companies, and skills (workers) moot with severe short-term consequences for all involved. Fluctuation in price, income/wealth, and credit determine who can and cannot consume regardless of their human needs. Although markets produce innovation and jobs (somewhere for someone), even Adam Smith (1776) acknowledged that markets cannot and do not keep people in mind, and therefore they must be tempered with moral regulations of fairness and justice.

That temperance is somewhat evident in President Obama's and Bill Gates' rhetorical representation and frame for CCS, but only the "powerful market" remains in the light of evidence. CCS ensures only that public schools will have continuous innovation and a redistribution of public resources to private businesses competing for market advantage with their focus on profit. And as Whitehurst (2009) and Loveless (2012) demonstrated, there is little reason to believe that innovation and profit will translate into more fair or just distributions of the benefits of schooling. So this is how we got here. The ideology of neoliberalism—with its faith in the market to solve all social problems—makes CCS a politically acceptable and economically feasible policy to address the problem of how to improve the performance of schools.

### But Is This the Way We Wish to Live Together?

Public schools could be and should be the American institution to promote fairness and justice; places where citizens learn to appreciate what markets can do and what they cannot do, what they have done and what they have not done. Part of this curriculum would be to understand the fact that markets are neither natural nor free (Chang 2010). They are a human artifact that people brought into existence, work to maintain, and are therefore changeable—if so desired. As Smith phrased it, markets can be and should be tempered in order to keep people in mind more often. After all, that's what an economy is supposed to be for in a democracy—to serve people's needs fairly and justly.

I want to believe that President Obama, Bill Gates, and other advocates of CCS believe this to be true as well. However, their neoliberal ideology ensures that we can't get there from here by forcing dispassionate market principles into schools—not through CCS and aligned systems (Loveless 2012), turnaround school improvement grants (Trujillo and Renee 2012), teacher financial incentives (Berry, Eckert, and Bauries 2012), charter schools (Baker and Ferris 2011; Miron, Urshchel, Mathis, and Tornquist 2010), or Teach for America (Heilig and Jez 2010). And we can't get there by subtracting the human caring from the curriculum, as David Coleman suggested when promoting CCS to the New York State Department of Education (2011b) and on Common Core Video Series / EngageNY (www.engageny.org/resource /common-core-video-series).

Before the New York State Department of Education, Coleman adopted a caustic tone, baiting the audience to name the most popular forms of writing in American high schools. Without citation or evidence, he reported exposition of personal opinion and presentation of personal matters as the most popular. He pardoned himself for speaking bluntly before explaining that grown people don't give a "shit" about how you think or feel. In the Engage NY video, Coleman used the same unsubstantiated claims, but substituted "cares" for his blunt remark. What they do care about, he argued—again without citation or evidence—is that you can make an argument with some warrants for your conclusions. He concluded his vignette before the NY Department of Education meeting by noting that personal writing will not help graduates when they are asked to write business reports later in life.

If Coleman's criterion were true, then no one should care for or accept the official argument for CCS because the only substantial evidence is that metaphorical business analysis concerning the CCS potential for a national market for new teaching and learning tools. Nor should teachers, students, and school communities accept the position of consumers that Gates offers them because there is little evidence that attests to the effectiveness of CCS, the examinations, or the tools to help all students learn more. And the only "something verifiable behind" the official argument is an opinion among powerful groups that the world and all that's in it should be run like a self-regulating market and that people are little more than human capital. The evidence of the Great Recession and its aftermath certainly brings that opinion into question here and around the world.

This lack of evidence for CCS opens spaces for teachers, students, and communities to step forward as agents in the ongoing development of school reform. Public schools do need reform based on ideologies that connect schoolwork with fairness and justice in our civil society (as well as with our economy). In Coleman's terms, these steps would demonstrate that teachers, students, and communities "give a shit" about the feelings, thoughts, and lives of all in America—particularly the circumstances of their childhoods. Caring about those circumstances refocuses reform on the imbalance in the learning outcomes among income segregated schools, but without the limitations of neoliberal ideology. While some of the content within the CCS might be helpful in this endeavor, there are forty years of failed neoliberal social policy to renegotiate as well. Reform of schooling must take place outside as well as inside schools. We all might ask the advocates of CCS, "What are your CCS for fairness and justice for our students' lives outside our classrooms?"

Former secretary of labor Robert Reich argues that such questions are necessary because

> Nothing good happens in Washington, or for that matter, in state capitals, unless good people outside Washington and those state capitals make it happen. Unless they push very hard. Unless they're organized, mobilized, and energized to force the political system to respond. (as quoted in Cook 2012, 36)

# CHAPTER 2

## *Common Core Children*

**>> RANDY BOMER**

*Who are we teaching?*

In some families, children are cast in the role of *future college student* before birth. There is language all around them from college-educated elders who never consider the possibility that the little ones are not bound for university—perhaps even the same institution their family members and ancestors attended. Many people reading these words may have come from such families, but they may be surprised to learn that they are a minority in the United States, where about 70 percent of adults do not have college degrees, even at a time when the rate of adults with bachelor degrees is at an all-time high (Pérez-Peña 2012b; U.S. Census Bureau 2012). In other families, like the one in which I grew up, children are positioned as deciders about their futures. The message is this: You'll choose whether you want to go to college, based on what you want to be and what you're interested in for your own life. In still other families, there cannot be an assumption of going to college, because no adults have attended and there is no extra money. In some of these families, the perspective toward college might be that, if a child really wants to go, everyone else will have to struggle to make that possible. In others, college is pretty unimaginable.

The Common Core State Standards (CCSS) mirror, amplify, and transpose onto all the children in the United States the position of children in that first kind of family. Every child, from kindergarten on, is positioned as a future college freshman. I'm sure we all agree that college access is important, and it is laudable to attempt to give all children a more equal start in being pre-pared for the gatekeeping first year of college. It is, however, a radical change in our thinking about children to assume that what will be available to be learned in school is limited to practicing to be a college freshman. But that is pretty close to the approach taken in the CCSS.

To understand why this is such a big change and a risky experiment, one has to consider the method by which these particular standards came into being. First, a set of "anchor standards" were developed, ones that aimed for some stereotypical assumptions about the literacy demands of the first year or so of college. The anchor standards are decidedly not based on the liter-acy demands of all four years of undergraduate experience, and certainly not professional or graduate school. The particular literacy demands of different disciplines, things college students do with words and texts as they progress in the higher levels of their major disciplines, are not addressed. Rather, the sole focus is a generic academic practice of making arguable points about texts and providing evidence from those texts. The false promise of such bland practices in academic writing has been documented in a whole li-brary's worth of research, theory, and practice about college level writing (e.g., Beaufort 2007; Sullivan and Tinberg 2006). We know that attempts, in first-year composition classes, to provide a generalized form of college reading and writing just do not transfer to students' experience as they move along in college and take on the practices of their majors. Furthermore, though the anchor standards advertised themselves as being for "college and career," there is in fact not a whisper about career-oriented writing in them. They should really be called "1951 freshman college reading and writing standards," because they are not really adequate representations of many of the things that college students do in 2013, much less people in the vast kaleidoscope of twenty-first-century careers.

At any rate, these anchor standards, which apply to graduating twelfth graders, are then dragged straight back through the grades all the way to early childhood. This is unusual in the history of making standards. In the past, standards writers (perhaps because they usually included teachers) did not say "if students have to do something in twelfth grade, we must plan how children do the same thing in kindergarten and then incrementally add complexity to that same practice across each year of school." That is, in the

CCSS, the way people grow up and learn. For example, CCSS Anchor Standard #1 for Writing asks that students "write arguments to support claims in an analysis of substantive topics or texts, using valid reasoning and relevant and sufficient evidence." Here is CCSS Reading Standard #1: "Read closely to determine what the text says explicitly and to make logical inferences from it; cite specific textual evidence when writing or speaking to support conclusions drawn from the text." Together, these two standards name a particular kind of reading that accompanies the corresponding specific form of writing. Clearly, a certain kind of literacy practice is being valued: A person is expected to read a text and then produce an original text that makes one or more references to the first textual object under discussion. The language being produced—a text about a text—is twice removed from concrete experience; the initial ideas come from a text, and the reader/writer is asked to reply with new thoughts about those initial thoughts—also in a text.

Lower grade standards, as I said, simply repeat the practice named in the anchor standard at simpler levels, as in Kindergarten Writing Standard #1: "Use a combination of drawing, dictating, and writing to compose opinion pieces in which they tell a reader the topic or the name of the book they are writing about and state an opinion or preference about the topic or book (e.g., My favorite book is . . . )." And here is First Grade Writing Standard #1: "Write opinion pieces in which they introduce the topic or name the book they are writing about, state an opinion, supply a reason for the opinion, and provide some sense of closure." In these standards for primary grades, the CCSS in fact ask young children to engage in essentially the same literacy practice as the one that is "college ready," albeit in a manner that makes sense with the ways young children compose—with drawings and oral language as well as writing. That is, they are asked to make a text about a text and provide evidence from the first text for what they claim in the second.

By contrast, teachers of young children tend to value children living through concrete experiences that they can then represent in signs; that tradition has been supported by much research across many disciplines. It is a radical break to assume that practices for college readiness should be engaged in beginning with five- and six-year-olds, a break that is not supported by one scintilla of research. No one has ever shown (or even attempted to show) that people will be more ready for college because they start in first grade making claims about texts and supporting them with evidence. In an era of accountability, however, teachers of young children have had to respond to wave after wave of what Hatch has called the "accountability shovedown" (Hatch 2002). The apparatus of accountability—high-stakes forms of assessment even in Head Start contexts—has increasingly put early childhood educators in the position of having to look away from a child's developmental trajectory and toward an abstracted goal that may not have anything to do with the present practices in which the child engages (Brown 2009, 2010; Goldstein 2007).

There is something—or someone—new being invented by this small group of people writing the standards. So who is this child? Who is the character being written into the story the standards tell about how people grow? And what are the ethics of treating children in this way?

## POSITIVE IDENTITIES FOR CHILDREN IN THE CCSS

I am going to be writing critically about some of the ways the CCSS position students, and about the roles in which children are cast in them. But it's also important to recognize some of the powerful and forward-looking identities opened up for children in these standards, and I want to name those roles here. First, and perhaps most importantly, the child in the standards is intellectually equal to all her/his peers—as able as anyone else to engage in the literacy practices required for that first year of college. The child, even at a young age, is assumed to be someone capable of more academic work than has often been asked of children. The standards insist that no one is incapable of growing into the kind of work sometimes thought to be typical of a first year of college; everyone will be good enough if they have a chance to learn.

Children composed in the collective imagination of the CCSS authors are readers with at least some thoughts beyond those given in the text (though not far beyond). On the one hand, there is quite a bit of concern expressed in the standards that children will think too much about their own experience in response to a text. The Third Grade Reading Standard #1, for instance, says, "Ask and answer questions to demonstrate understanding of a text, referring explicitly to the text as the basis for the answers." On the other hand, there is some indication that children will be thinking actively about a text and drawing some ideas from it, such as Third Grade Reading Standard #6: "Distinguish their own point of view from that of the narrator or those of the characters." This, at least, positions students as independent thinkers more than anything in the National Reading Panel Report (National Institute of Child Health and Human Development 2000) or the policies derived from it. So compared to phonics drills, worksheets, or reductive factual knowledge questions, the child in the CCSS is somewhat more of a responsive reader. Even in the first grade, students are expected to go beyond the stark behaviorism of Reading First when they are asked to "describe the connection between two individuals, events, ideas, or pieces of information in a text" (RI.1.3) and to "identify the reasons an author gives to support points in a text" (RI.1.8). A person constructed to do these things is clearly positioned as more thoughtful and responsive than someone being shaped just to develop habitual automaticity of decoding graphemes into phonemes. To be sure, this is not Louise Rosenblatt ([1978] 1994), but the child is occasionally assumed to be someone capable of saying something *about* a text, not just to perform it out loud and answer simple questions about it.

The child writers constructed by the CCSS are people who actually compose, who create whole texts. While the range of composing they are assumed to be doing is narrower than the luckiest students in America, it is at least composing, and that will be a change for the relatively unlucky students who are never asked to compose anything. Anyone familiar with the range of "writing" practices in elementary schools, who is not limited in their perspective only to schools attempting the practices valued by many readers of this book, will be aware that children are not always assumed to be composers of whole texts. It is still common for children to be asked to copy text from something the teacher has written or projected in the front of the room. It is still common in elementary schools for children to write no more than a brief phrase in response to a question. The children in such contexts will be rewritten as their schools and teachers attempt to take on the practices required in the CCSS. An identity of *maker of texts* will become available, even required, and that is something to celebrate.

One other identity that the CCSS make *almost but not quite* available to children is that of a participant in a public conversation about texts, content, and ideas. When the standards ask that children be able to refer to textual evidence, that's a step toward being able to discuss with others what they see, explain with reference to shared material why they see it as they do, and enter into negotiations about meanings. The trouble is that the standards never get very close to the actual social work of convincing others or negotiating; they remain stuck at the testable behavior of citing textual evidence, without the motivating and meaning-giving context of actually sharing with others through talk or writing. (The CCSS were mostly composed by people from the testing industry, with a clear commitment to framing expectations in ways that could be easily assessed with tests.) However, if teachers choose to work on these evidence-oriented standards with students in a way that involves student-to-student persuasion and negotiation, an identity of public participant becomes available to children, and that identity is important to citizenship in a democracy, as well as being important in higher education and many other lifelong learning contexts. Once again, this is an identity that has rarely been afforded to children, and it would be valuable to have it more widely distributed.

## CRITIQUE OF HOW CCSS POSITION CHILDREN

To critique the CCSS is not to be unfriendly, complaining, or curmudgeonly. It is to be critical—to recognize that political artifacts, such as standards for public schools, always encode relations of power. Being critical means exposing who wins and loses in those relations, and insisting that there are alternatives. It's especially important to critique the standards because, by their nature, they standardize; they narrow the possible practices and identities available to students. Whether or not this narrowing is justified as national policy (and I think it is not), it falls to teachers and schools to restore at least some of the possibilities that have been repressed in this authoritative set of documents. It is good that the Common Core is, supposedly, intended to be just a core—not the whole fruit. Let's keep in mind that some fruits (say, mangos) have a gigantic core, so that it's hard for people who haven't had a lot of practice to get to the good part. Other fruits (say, pears) have a small core and ample deliciousness all around it. By being aware of the limitations in the standards, maybe teachers can build up the deliciousness in what's available to students to learn and the possible selves that those practices may carry with them.

## Limits on Possibility

I showed at the start of this chapter that the CCSS, right down to kindergarten, position children as college-freshmen-in-training. The form of literacy—and the identity that accompanies it—that K–12 schooling values and encourages is limited to a set of practices that are native to a very particular location in society.

For everyone, even those individuals who are wonderful at being college freshmen, it is at most a very temporary, transitory identity—let's say it lasts two years or so for those who ever take it on at all. After that, most of those people take on many new literate identities and leave behind things like finding a focused but arguable thesis, arranging arguments about texts in logical order, and providing textual evidence for their reasoning about the text under discussion. The ways people do these things in chemistry, as they progress into the major, are different from the ways they write in art history, and different still from the writing practices of pharmacology. All of these are also part of a college experience. And the college experience, even for those of us who extend it as far as possible into graduate school, is relatively brief. Life, however, is long.

But what about the people who do not complete high school—20 to 30 percent of those who begin high school? What will their literacy education have provided them? Aren't they entitled to an education that is useful and meaningful to some parts of their lives? And will the preparation for early college experiences have seemed worth their whole childhoods for those people—around half of entering students—who do not complete a four-year college degree? What will they think all that was for? Even for the college graduates who go on to careers in business, engineering, or music, is it legitimate to have narrowed the goals of all their earlier schooling to this slim band of practices that are native only to a very short time in their lives? Why was their education only relevant to *one* of the many selves they take on, even by the end of college?

After all, even in the college years, people use literacy for purposes that go well beyond schooling. In their study of undergraduates at Stanford University, Fishman and her colleagues (Fishman, Lunsford, McGregor, and Otuteye 2005) found that college students have rich and diverse literate lives outside the classroom and that, in fact, their outside-school practices help them to get over the insults to their confidence that they often experience in the first year of college. Many first-year college students start to think they can't control writing at all, but it's their participation in a wider array of writing practices that helps them regather their confidence (and remember, these are students at an elite university). For example, the reading and writing they did as performers—in such activities as theatre productions and performance poetry—were important to their success as college students. Neither Fishman's informants—nor, I wager, anyone else—ever said they would have benefitted as college students if they had been making more evidence-based claims about texts in kindergarten and first grade. Rather, college students—like, one would hope, children—draw upon diverse experiences in their self-composition as readers and writers. Fishman and her colleagues have shown clearly that students pull together multiple, complex identities in order to become capable users of literacy for college. And of course, for life beyond the first two years of college, it's even more important that people assume many different identity positions in order to take advantage of the full range of uses of writing and the shapes it takes within other social practices.

Literacy is liquid; its meaning takes the shape of its container. The practices imposed on college freshmen are only one shaping context. We always read or write as part of other activity as we assume identities that often have very little to do with reading and writing as such. We write and read as friends, to keep in touch; as spiritual questers, to meditate, pray, reach for what seems best and highest, and to figure out how best to live. We write and read as artists, to make and participate in creating something beautiful. We write as organizers, to coordinate activity with other people, to plan what will happen, and to document what has occurred. We read and write as activists, to imagine how the world can be better, to influence our communities, to create political coalitions, and to change social givens. Even when we are performing as students, we write more than those familiar persuasive essays in which a generalized claim is supported by reasons and evidence; we reflect, make new ideas, record information, and manage our activity. None of these is touched in the CCSS, which offer children this possible future practice: reading texts in order to write essays about them, in which they prove they are right by providing evidence from the text they have read. It is hazardously flimsy support for a literate life.

## Suspicious Regard

Every person reading this knows kids whose parents don't trust them. Call these kids' names, and they look up, wide-eyed, staring guiltily, already assuming they're in trouble. They monitor the responses of any nearby adult for approval or disapproval. They seem unable just to assume that their actions or statements are going to be OK. I am not suggesting we necessarily blame parents, teachers, or anyone else for every case of this kind of paranoia. I only want to say here that, if a child is often regarded with suspicion, she/he reasonably comes to mistrust her/his own impulses and ideas. She/he has been positioned as suspect, and that position is one of the main things in her/his environment that is available to be learned. It is in the curriculum.

In both reading and writing, the CCSS fixate and obsess upon children providing evidence. The word "evidence" is used 136 times in the standards, and in 133 of those instances it is something that students are expected to provide. Children's assertions are never supposed to be taken at face value. This relationship is actually quite strange in most U.S. cultures, because most adult-child interactions take children's utterances as acceptable statements without evidence, as providing information about how the child sees the world. But in the CCSS, children always need to show where it is in the book, to ground their claims in other people's reasoning and language. Now I'm not going to pretend that this is a total shock; it is a common academic ambition to try to force students to pay attention to what is not already in their minds, to attend to what is new and authoritative, so that they outgrow their current knowledge. But 133 uses of the term is a lot, and it seems to indicate that evidence is highly valued indeed in this culture of ours.

That's curious, because there is no evidence provided in the CCSS for their own assertions that this curricular architecture—especially the perseverant teaching of the same standards across all of school—will do anything to help children gain access to the gleaming future of college and career that the makers of the standards seem to promise. If evidence is so important for eight-year-olds, why is there no evidence (and none exists) for the standards? The answer is that evidence is rarely required and very often completely ignored in our society.

In actual fact, huge numbers of people don't think evidence is very important at all unless it confirms what they already think. This is even true of professionals in public media. You would think that would be one of the few careers that would likely really employ standards of evidence. Recently, the entire sports media establishment reported that a college football player had met and fallen in love with a girl, that she had been in a terrible car accident, and that she later died. Professional writers in major newspapers, magazines, and media outlets reported all of these things, even though the girl never existed at all. These were all college educated journalists, and surely an example of people whose careers depend upon providing evidence. Not only did they not provide the evidence in their writing; they did not even look at evidence for themselves. If they were in the fourth grade, though, and in a classroom dominated by the values enshrined in the CCSS, they would have to provide evidence every time they wanted to talk about the reasons a character in a story did something.

In our own field of education, a woman with a doctoral degree, Ruby Payne, has sold 1.5 million copies of a book she wrote that makes nearly two hundred claims about poor children, their families, and their communities (Payne 2005). There is no evidence for almost any of these claims (Bomer, Dworin, May, and Semingson 2008). She does not provide any evidence in the book, and that has not hurt her sales to millions of educators with college degrees and careers. Not only that, when *New York Times* journalist and editor Paul Tough investigated Payne and the claims her critics have made about her, he wrote, "You would think that Payne wouldn't fret about a few angry assistant professors whose collective audience is a tiny fraction of the size of hers" (Tough 2007). Tough, a powerful and highly influential person in the information economy, took no interest in evidence (indeed seemed to ridicule the people who did attend to evidence) but rather took Payne's celebrity as evidence of the quality of her claims. But children in school have to take evidence very, very seriously. Does this sound like a culture that values evidence? It sounds to me as if people who occupy powerful positions can say anything they want, ignoring any need for substantiation, while even very small school children had better consider themselves perpetually in a court of law with very high standards of evidence.

## Instrumental Texts, Instrumental Lives

Children, as designed by the CCSS authors, should take the texts they read as objects to use in demonstrations of their mastery of the standards—as things to use to show they're learning to do as they are told. A novel is never simply a world to get lost in, or a journey of self-discovery, or an experience of beauty and insight. They are never supposed to read a nonfiction text about insects and simply reflect on biodiversity, marvel at creation, or just set it down, saying, "Huh, that was interesting." The child reader in these standards is supposed to take texts as things to be used; the relationship to the word is shaped as an instrumental one. Children (all of them) are expected to become people who aren't too strongly moved by anything, who can't be transformed or even thrown off course, but rather are clinical and analytic—cool customers, ready to stand and deliver their thoughts and evidence.

Similarly, both the standards and the government entities that have sponsored them and granted them such authority have taken an instrumental stance toward the lives of children. Children are destined to become college educated because that is what is needed in America's workforce for the nation to be globally competitive. This use of human lives as instruments for the economy is part of a political posture known as neoliberalism, and it treats people as a type of exploitable resource, like petroleum or timber. When policy makers, like those who composed the CCSS, are seized by neoliberalism, it never seems to occur to them that it has long been a principle of moral philosophy that people cannot be treated as means to an end. People are supposed to be treated as ends in themselves, as intrinsically valuable because of their personhood, not as an instrument to achieve something else—like economic advancement for the nation.

I don't think it is terribly unusual for people to take their own children as ends in themselves. Parents know their kids are different, that their futures will be determined out of their own interests, loves, and personalities. I suspect even the people who argue most strongly for the virtues of the CCSS view their own children that way. But too often, when they take "school children" as a category, it becomes tempting to play social engineer and to write for the nation's children a life story that no one would particularly desire for their own.

# CHAPTER 3

## *Texts and Teens: Separate and Unequal*

>> M A J A   W I L S O N

*Why do we read?*

I might consider the Common Core Reading Standards (CCRS) relatively harmless—if I read them out of context. But when I account for the intentions of their authors and the system of accountability that gives them meaning, I understand them differently. The Reading Standards attempt to separate students' experiences and feelings from the texts that they read. Perpetrating a cynical and controlling view of children and citizens, this separation creates an unequal relationship between teens and texts that serves the interests of the already powerful.

But before we explore how the Reading Standards position teens in relation to texts, let's consider the kind of relationship I want all my students—and my two adolescent sons—to have with reading.

Picture a twelve-year-old boy as he confronts a word he doesn't understand: *abolition.* This boy is a precocious reader, and if he'd been born in the twenty-first century, we might imagine him sitting at a desk as his class reads *Narrative of the Life of Frederick Douglass,* a Common Core exemplar text listed for eighth graders by the education company founded by CCSS author David Coleman (www.achievethecore.org). But our twelve-year-old wasn't born in this century.

It is sometime in the 1820s, and this boy isn't *reading* Frederick Douglass; he *is* Frederick Douglass. Years before he will pen his autobiography or forge his own pass to freedom, Douglass is deep in the midst of an existential crisis triggered by his newly won ability to read. He's already read and re-read a dialogue between an escaped slave and his master in *The Columbian Orator*, finding that it "gave tongue to interesting thoughts of my own soul" (1845, 34–35). But these thoughts have become an unbearable torment, and he sometimes wishes he'd never learned to read. He sometimes even wishes himself dead: "Anything, no matter what, to get rid of the thinking!" (35).

Douglass isn't sitting in a classroom and there's no one he can ask to help him understand what *abolition* means. The dictionary's circular definition—*to abolish something*—is no help. But he's determined to figure it out. He's heard the word before, every time a slave's attempt to escape is blamed on "the fruits of *abolition*." His struggle with literacy has always been deeply personal, and the weight of his experiences and despair hang on his understanding of this word. So he waits, biding his time until he locates a newspaper reporting on northern petitions for the abolition of slavery. Now he understands, and he develops a plan: "Meanwhile, I would learn to write" (37).

Douglass' struggle to comprehend this single word embodies the relationship I want all my students to have with text: intensely personal, fiercely dynamic, nested deeply within experience, with the potential to disrupt established hierarchies. This kind of relationship led me to teach reading and writing in the first place. And this kind of personally engaged reading is precisely what the CCRS attempt to prevent.

## THE STANDARDS DOCUMENT ITSELF

It is difficult to figure out how the CCRS position adolescents in relation to texts—when we read them in isolation. The standards are vague enough that we can read a range of teaching practices and relational schemes into them. Consider the first "anchor" for the sixth- to twelfth-grade Reading Standards:

> Read closely to determine what the text says explicitly and to make logical inferences from it; cite specific textual evidence when writing or speaking to support conclusions drawn from the text. (CCSI 35)

This sentence doesn't give me pause; I can read my own writing, reading, and teaching practices into it. But, as every good English teacher knows, context matters.

This single sentence, like any artifact of human activity, exists within a complicated relational web of people, ideas, and systems. To understand and predict the practical consequences of this standard in the lives of adolescent readers, we have to understand how it is positioned within this web. We must step outside the standards document, in other words, to comprehend it. And straying outside the "four corners" of any text is precisely what the authors of the CCRS don't want any of us to do.

## THE STANDARDS IN CONTEXT: AUTHORIAL INTENTION OBSCURED, EXPRESSED, AND ENFORCED

To understand the standards, it helps to understand the perspectives of the authors who wrote them. This is trickier—by design—than it would seem. The standards document doesn't give its authors a byline. There is no vestige of their presence in its language, no *I* or *we* to make the reader wonder about the human beings whose life experiences, beliefs, and purposes shaped them.

There's a good rhetorical reason for the authors' absence, beyond the usual explanation that technical documents represent the views of the organizations that sponsor them, not the individuals who wrote them. To generate the support of the nation's educators and policy makers, the authors obscured their authorial role to create the illusion that the standards emerged from widespread professional consensus. There's a similar strategic reason for the standards' vagueness: if educators whose beliefs and practices conflicted with the authors' intentions could read their own purposes into the standards (like I did), then they'd be more likely to support—or not actively work against—their adoption.

But once the majority of states had adopted the standards (threatened with the promise of RTTT funds), the authors made their presence known, expressing and enforcing their intentions in a variety of ways. We get a very consistent picture of these intentions—and how they position students and texts in relation to one another—through two snapshots of the authors' views, all taken after the standards' adoption.

## Snapshot One

David Liben, a member of the English Language Arts (ELA) Standards Working Group, expressed his authorial intention in a workshop devoted to aligning basal readers to the CCSS. Catherine Gewertz reported Liben's comments in April of 2012:

> [David Liben] reminded the participants that the common standards "virtually eliminate text-to-self connections," meaning they focus on getting students to figure out what the text means, rather than how they feel about it. That, he said, better prepares them for college and jobs. "In college and careers, no one cares how you feel," Mr. Liben said. "Imagine being asked to write a memo on why your company's stock price has plummeted: 'Analyze why and tell me how you feel about it,'" he said. (Gewertz 2012)

It is easy to write off Liben's comment as a slip of the tongue. But, again, we must take Liben's comments in context: they echo David Coleman's. In 2011, in front of the New York Departement of Education (DOE), Coleman made this assertion: that students in the nation's high schools spend most of their time on writing projects that involve the "presentation of a personal matter" and the "exposition of a personal opinion." In support of this assertion, he presented the same anecdotal evidence Liben would later offer: employers don't ask for a "compelling account of your childhood" before asking for a market analysis. And, in a line that has since gone viral on education blogs but that he refused to grant Heinemann permission to reprint here, Coleman used a word that starts with "s" and rhymes with "it" (and would mortify all our grandmothers) to sum up his thoughts and feelings: growing up involves the realization that people don't give a poop about your thoughts and feelings.

Coleman's and Liben's comments are similar enough to have been rehearsed or at least discussed, perhaps as they participated in the same ELA

Standards Working Group. Therefore, we have to take them into account as we try to comprehend the reading standards.

The logic in these comments is based on the same string of bad assumptions. Even if we accept the debatable assumption that the primary goal of education is to prepare children for the workplace, and even if we accept the morally deficient assumption that a hypothetical professor's or boss's disregard for a child's future feelings justifies our disregard for her/his present feelings, it is impossible for an informed person to accept this assertion about college and the workplace: "No one cares how you feel." It just isn't true.

Universities care how students feel for both humane and pragmatic reasons: students' mental and emotional well-being directly affects their ability to learn and stay in school—and, thus, the school's reputation and bottom line. Universities devote tremendous resources to campus climate. The Division of Student Affairs (DSA) at my own university helps students find and make community within the larger university, provides hazing education and prevention initiatives, and directs students to campus mental health for free counseling services. The University of Maine's DSA 170-word mission statement makes these references to students' feelings: "student satisfaction"; "community that nurtures . . . [students] in realizing their . . . personal potential"; "[student] interests and needs," and "emotional safety."

Concern within universities for students' feelings isn't limited to the realm of social adjustment. In 2003, composition researchers Marcia Curtis and Anne Herrington studied the writing development of four students across four years of college, concluding that the overtly personal writing these students were asked to do in first-year composition classes connected in striking ways to the development and direction of their disciplinary interests—even though the personal origins of these academic interests were increasingly obscured in the disciplinary conventions of their later work:

> In her first-year research essay, titled "The Psychological Effects of Child Abuse," Rachel, for instance, working through successive drafts, used successively her named-self, a pseudonymous-self, and finally an acquaintance as sample subject. . . . Nearly four

years later, she completed her honors thesis for psychology, "Intimacy Issues Among Young Adults: A Study of Family Alcoholism and Its Effects upon Children." Undeniably subject-focused and other-directed, Rachel's senior project was also undeniably tied to that first-year essay and Rachel's own initial subject place within it. (72)

If Curtis and Herrington's findings apply beyond the four students they studied, then Coleman's and Liben's assertions and assumptions aren't just unsupported, they're counter-indicated. If teachers act on Coleman's and Liben's assumptions, redesigning literacy curricula to keep students' thoughts and feelings at arm's length from the texts they read and compose, they'll undermine students' ability to forge productive connections between their experiences, the texts they read and write, and their emerging academic and career commitments. In other words, even if future participation within academic or professional communities requires members to subsume their experiences, thoughts, and feelings, Curtis and Herrington's study indicates that full and meaningful participation within these communities is better achieved by *exploring* rather than by ignoring those experiences.

Coleman and Liben aren't even right that no one cares what you think or feel in the workplace. Antiharassment legislation represents a national interest in how workers feel. There's an entire industry devoted to "employee morale." And business researchers deal frequently with the question of how relationships between bosses and employees affect employees' feelings—and, thus, productivity. Consider this study on bosses' introversion. Researchers found that when members of work teams expressed strong opinions about how to perform a task, teams with introverted leaders performed 14 percent better than teams with extroverted leaders because "the introverted leaders listened carefully and made employees feel valued" (Grant, Gino, and Hoffman 2010). Everyone but Liben seems to know that good bosses care what their employees think and feel. Not all bosses act on this knowledge. Perhaps Coleman and Liben have experienced or *been* such bosses themselves. But most of us, including the researchers, call them "bad bosses."

Why should any of us give a shit what Coleman or Liben think about the role of text-to-self connections in reading? Despite the unfounded assertions and bad assumptions, their thoughts, feelings, and assumptions do matter. Coleman and Liben are in positions of power, positions that also exist within a larger context: the punitive system of accountability that gives the standards their practical punch. The CCSS exist to feed the accountability machine—a machine designed to control public schools and teachers by doling out punishments and rewards in the form of funding and autonomy. The formulas for determining who gets what don't work without the numbers generated by standardized tests. And the tests can't be created without the standards on which they're based.

So in addition to the power vested in these authors by their role in authoring the standards, Coleman is positioned to ensure that their intentions for the standards will be embedded in the assessments. In early 2012, he was named president of the College Board, the parent organization of Educational Testing Services (ETS), declaring his goal in this position: to align the SAT to *his* version of the Common Core (Gewertz 2012a). Thus, even though the "virtual elimination" of text-to-self or text-to-world connections is never explicitly stated within the standards document, Coleman is in a position to enforce their elimination.

## Snapshot Two

Here's another way in which both Liben and Coleman have positioned themselves to directly affect the way that the standards are interpreted in classrooms across the country—through their role in shaping textbooks. This influence doesn't end with the group gathered with Liben to eliminate text-to-self connections from basal readers. It extends to all the major textbook companies that consult the *Publisher's Criteria for the Common Core State Standards in English Language Arts* (2011), funded by the Gates Foundation and authored by David Coleman and Susan Pimentel.

We can dismiss Coleman's and Liben's comments if we wish, but we can't dismiss the *Criteria*, which will shape the teaching of the hundreds of thousands of teachers who rely, by choice or mandate, on textbooks. The *Criteria*, which dictates what publishers should and should *not* include in their curricular materials, contains a curious motif: "the text itself" (2011, 1). That the word "text" would appear repeatedly in this document is unremarkable. But the attachment of the emphatic "itself" seven times to the word "text" *is* remarkable: it isn't as if the word "text" needs emphasis in a sixteen-page text with approximately three hundred mentions of texts.

Here's why all the emphatic emphasis: Coleman and Pimentel are tired of teachers who emphasize the reader's role in creating meaning. Throughout the *Criteria*, textbook publishers are enjoined to eliminate questions, materials, or activities that do not focus on "the text itself." In case there is any question about how much focus on the text itself is enough, a percentage is given: "Eighty to 90 percent" (2011, 6). This emphasis is attributed to the same standard I confessed reading my own teaching practices into—Reading Standard #1. According to Coleman and Pimentel,

> The Common Core State Standards place a high priority on the close, sustained reading of complex text, beginning with Reading Standard 1. Such reading . . . strives to focus on what lies within the four corners of the text. (2011, 4)

How to understand what Coleman and Pimentel mean here by "focus on what lies within the four corners of the text"? Coleman's and Liben's earlier comments join a later sentence from the *Criteria* to provide the context we need for our reading of this phrase:

> The Common Core State Standards call for students to demonstrate a careful understanding of what they read before engaging their opinions, appraisals, or interpretations.[1] (2011, 7)

---

1. In a revision of the *Criteria* completed almost a year after the first draft was released, Coleman and Pimentel hedge, adding this sentence to a discussion of the questions that should be asked of students before, during, and after reading: "student background knowledge and experiences can illuminate the reading but should not replace attention to the text itself" (2012, 16). But this hedge does nothing to shift the focus in the *Criteria* in any significant way. For example, this sentence comes two paragraphs after the following injunction: "text-dependent questions [which must comprise 80 to 90 percent of the analysis done by students, and, therefore, 80 to 90 percent of the questions posed by textbook publishers] do not require information or evidence from outside the text or texts" (2012, 5). In other words, the model of reading represented in both versions of the *Criteria* is exactly the same: while experiences and feelings may be applied to the analysis *after* reading and full comprehension have taken place, they should play no role in helping students to read and comprehend in the first place.

# TEENS AND TEXTS: SEPARATE AND *NOT* EQUAL

Liben, Pimentel, and Coleman's intentions for the reading standards—that teachers should require students to fully comprehend texts *without* engaging their experiences, thoughts, and opinions—finally shows us how the Reading Standards position adolescents in relationship with texts. They do not envision an equal relationship between teens and texts. In an equal relationship, the experiences of both parties are brought to bear on the interaction—the transaction between text and reader that Louise Rosenblatt spent her career describing. Instead, Liben, Pimentel, and Coleman position the student as subservient to the text: their connections are brought to bear only after the student has submitted to its authority, fully comprehending the text on its own terms. The "text itself" is the authority: its meaning must be divined and not constructed by students. After all, when it comes to students and the workers that Liben and Coleman expect them to become, "people really don't give a shit about what you feel or what you think."

Of course, this view isn't just immoral; it is highly impractical. I spent five years of my ten-year secondary public school career teaching in two different alternative education programs. Most of my students had failed or dropped out of the traditional system—or been kicked out of it. Engaging them in reading *any* text—let alone the "challenging texts" called for by the Reading Standards—was challenging work. There are two basic models for working with such students: You can puff up your chest, raise your voice, and rely on an ever-escalating system of rewards and punishments to control their actions; or you can work to persuade them through the learning experiences you structure that the work you are trying to engage them in will help them to resolve the conflicts in their lives that drive them to anger and despair, not to mention difficulty with school. Good luck with the former.

I chose the latter, and engaged my students in texts by directly engaging their experiences, thoughts, and feelings. I moved back and forth between students' experiences and what we were reading, comparing the text (and its various contexts) to the predictions and interpretations they'd constructed. But if I hadn't purposefully engaged my students' experiences and feelings from the beginning, I never would have succeeded in getting them to read, much less comprehend, anything.

There may be various underlying reasons for Coleman, Pimentel, and Liben's desire to keep adolescents' thoughts, feelings, and opinions at arm's length: they may fear adolescents; they may find their thoughts and feelings messy and offensive; they may simply not have much patience for adolescents' sometimes self-focused energy. But there is surely another reason for the standards' attempts to separate readers' feelings and thoughts from their readings, positioning them as subservient to the text itself.

The system of accountability in which Coleman, Pimentel, and Liben have positioned themselves is a system that seeks to control others—not to persuade them in and through relationships and democratic procedures, but to control them through a system of rewards and punishments with the weight of law behind it. There are many such smaller systems in schools, some chosen voluntarily by teachers to control the behavior of their students. But there are, in this country, no systems of control quite so large, quite so public, and quite so consequential as this—a nationwide system of accountability designed to control the lynchpin of a democracy, its public schools.

One way to ensure that the effects of this controlling system last long after students have left school is to prevent them from developing a relationship with the liberatory power of literacy. As Douglass knew, personally engaged readers have the potential to disrupt established hierarchies. Do those positioned at the top of these hierarchies—such as Coleman—really *want* to encourage the full, transformative power of literacy? The answer to that question should be painfully clear by now. Of course, as Douglass showed us, it is impossible even for the most controlling master, backed by the laws of the land, to stand between a boy and the books he knows hold the key to his freedom.

Some children, like Douglass, will form powerful relationships with literacy no matter what teachers or policy makers do. The question for educators is this: will the children in our classrooms form powerful relationships with literacy despite us, or with our help? Answering that question may require that we disrupt established hierarchies ourselves. But the stakes are high, and we can't say we don't know better: literature has given us such glorious exemplars.

# CHAPTER 4

## Understanding Digital and Media Texts in the Common Core

>> PEGGY ALBERS

*Whose text is it anyway?*

In 1980, Brian Clark wrote a play entitled *Whose Life Is It Anyway?* This play focuses on sculptor Ken Harrison, who gets into a car accident that results in his quadriplegia. Knowing he will never sculpt again and seeing that his life as he knows it is over, Harrison wishes to die with dignity, and works diligently to convince others that his decision is rational. Throughout the play, Clark presents arguments for and against Harrison's wish; by doing so, he positions the audience to consider to what extent the government and the law should be allowed to interfere in the lives of private citizens.

As an academic who is also a practicing artist, I am committed at the deepest level to the role of visual and digital texts in schooling and how they critically shape who we are. Across the years, I have studied visual and media texts interpreted and created in school settings. Within this body of work, I have argued that attention must be paid to the visual and digital texts created by students, as these texts make visible the beliefs and values that underpin decisions behind their design and content choices (Albers 2011). What my work has attempted to do is to place significance on the role of the visual and digital as it operates within the everyday, and critically attend to how and what texts mean; the complexity of the choices that emerge within these texts; and the nature of reading, interpreting, and producing these challenging texts. My essay draws upon Clark's play as analogous to the role that the Common Core State Standards (CCSS) have and will play in the decision making of schools, districts, counties, and (of course) teachers and students themselves. More specifically, this chapter questions the CCSS's definitions of text, text complexity, and readers; probes how these terms are framed in the CCSS; and argues for significant attention to how text is read, interpreted, and produced in twenty-first-century classes.

## WHOSE TEXT IS COMPLEX ANYWAY?

What it means to be literate continually shifts in its complexities as new technologies surface, and these tools enable people to shape texts as much as these texts shape us. In twenty-first-century literacies, all semiotic systems and objects as artifacts of our literacy practices are understood as "texts" that, and in today's world, must be understood as carrying significance. Film, video, clothing, body, food, images, dance, and so on are considered texts. Within each text are modes (e.g., visual, aural, spatial, and gestural) that communicate part of the message; some modes carry more of the message than others. The meanings that underpin these texts (as well as written texts) are culturally situated, negotiated, and interpreted not just through schools, but in our everyday lives (Shannon 2011).

For twenty years, I have systematically studied school-generated texts created across age groups and have developed a taxonomy around how to analyze these texts (Albers 2007). In 2004, I published an article that included a photo of a large papier-mâché figure of an African American male created by Barry, a twelve-year-old white male—an image that haunts me still.

Barry's design and content choices reflected his knowledge of media and art (e.g., shape, color, proportion) and his beliefs and values reflecting the racism historically and culturally deeply situated in this community. The figure (visual mode) had a red slash across its neck, and its tongue dangling in the middle of its upturned (as in a smile) mouth. Its severed arms are represented by bloodied sockets painted in red tempera. When Barry presented his text in class, students were unaffected by its racist message; however, the teacher used this text to design curricular engagements to disrupt racist assumptions held by many of these sixth-grade students. Barry's text emerged from the intertextual interplay of his design and content choices, his family and community beliefs and practices, and his previous readings of a range of texts (image, written, video, performance). These tracings of his learning and social practices were made visible in this highly complex message of hate.

I use this example to suggest that what "text" actually is and/or means is not simple; "text" has many complex and intricate meanings. Texts are in a dialectal relation with context; the text creates the context as much as the context creates the text (Halliday 1978). Meaning arises from the friction between the two. Fish (1980) suggests that "text" is located in the reader, "is not a spatial object but an occasion for a temporal experience" (345), and that temporal reading depends on the structure of the reading experience. It is this experience that produces the "text." In Fish's perspective, a text is never stable, but is dependent on the time, place, and context of the reading. As such, "text" has innumerable representations, none being any more significant, complex, or challenging than another; it is the context and the reader that create the complexity.

As represented in the CCSS, text is narrowly characterized through written language, and defines "complexity" in terms of sentence length and structure, cohesion, vocabulary, organization, and background knowledge (Shanahan, Fisher, and Frey 2012). Adams (2009) writes, "There may be one day modes and methods of information delivery that are as efficient and powerful as text, but for now there is no contest. To grow, our students must read lots, and more specifically, they must read lots of 'complex' texts—texts that offer them new language, new knowledge, and new modes of thought" (National Governors Association 2010, as cited in Appendix A, 4). I argue that when texts are defined more broadly as explained above, students read and experience "lots" of complex texts in the shape of images, photographs, icons, music, websites, and so on. Significant texts like Maya Lin's *Vietnam Veterans Memorial* or Steven Spielberg's *Schindler's List* or Cleve Jones's *AIDS Memorial Quilt* have impacted the world powerfully through visual, musical, cinematic, and textile modes, respectively. To suggest that no other modes carry information efficiently and powerfully is shortsighted, naïve, and print-centric.

# WHOSE AMERICA'S NEXT TOP MODEL ANYWAY?

America is obsessed with models, examples and demonstrations of how to act, look, behave, talk, educate, and so on. We live in an "appearance culture," a culture that values and sets ideals for cultural models of beauty and body shape (Vilhjalmsson, Kristjansdottir, and Ward 2012). According to Gee (1999), cultural models, "images or storylines or descriptions," are based on the "taken-for-granted assumptions about what is 'typical' or 'normal'" (59). Within an appearance culture, prescribed notions of normative ideal body shapes are generated, framed in such a way that people from young children through adults aspire—often at great cost (e.g., financial, physical, emotional)—to have this shape (Hill 2009). The CCSS three-tiered model of measuring text complexity follows this trend, especially in how it has defined complex and challenging text.

### Think of a Portrait

In describing itself, the CCSS want us to consider its descriptions "not as standards themselves but" to show "portraits of students who meet the standards set out in this document" (National Governors Association 2010, as cited in Appendix A, 4). When we hear or read the word "portrait," its frame or collection of frames (Lakoff 2004) is activated in our brains, and shapes the way we view that particular concept, idea, and object. "Portrait" as a metaphor appeals to the aesthetic, something pleasing. The descriptions about student expectations are framed as pleasing, positive, and enriching. As a conceptual construct (Lakoff and Johnson 2003), the CCSS as "portrait" is equated to a beautiful piece of art—classic, traditional, historically and critically recognized, significant, an object with "staying power." As a physical object, a portrait often symbolizes wealth and models of success (e.g., royalty, presidents, CEOs, celebrities). A "portrait of students who meet the standards" is a pleasing picture of American students who, collectively, "read lots, and more specifically . . . lots of 'complex' texts" (Adams 2009, as cited in Appendix A, 4). They are held up as virtual models of success, the "ideal," and will define "the norm." This "portrait of students" represents the "face" of what the CCSS hopes will be the typical American reader (Figure 4.1).

Copyright 2013   tagxedo.com

**Figure 4.1** Portrait of Text Complexity: Tagxedo Created from CCSS Statements, 7.

The frames activated by the word "standard" most likely have a more negative connotation, or appearance, and elicit unpleasant thoughts for educators (e.g., Race To The Top, Dynamic Indicators of Basic Early Literacy Skills [DIBELS], deprofessionalization of teachers). My point is if student expectations are framed as a "portrait," the CCSS and the definitions of text, reading, and readers become almost pleasing in comparison to "standards"; many will believe they are "not so bad." However, still lurking in the midst are antiquated concepts of text. The CCSS definitions and examples of text complexity will become central to instruction and curriculum at the expense of twenty-first-century texts and twenty-first-century students.

If "complex" texts are framed in terms of written text, it is no surprise that the everyday texts of twenty-first-century students, "videos, podcasts, and tweets" (National Governors Association 2010, Appendix A, 4) take on metaphors that have negative connotations—"text light" and "text free," texts framed as the antithesis of complexity, antimodels so to speak. They are "light" or "free" because they "cannot capture the nuance, subtlety, depth, or breadth of ideas developed through complex text" (National Governors Association 2010, Appendix A, 4). As marketing concepts for the diet industry, "light" and "fat free" are directly associated with and central to appearance (weight loss, change in body shape). Billions are spent in advertising (commercials, images, tweets, videos, podcasts) convincing consumers through "text light" or "text free" sources to buy and buy into their product line. By using these two concepts, the CCSS signals that the appearance of the text, and thus American students, is everything. Reading, creating, and integrating text-light texts into instruction most likely means that American students "cannot read complex expository text to gain information" (National Governors Association 2010, Appendix A, 4). The CCSS is, in essence, selling its definition of challenging text by juxtaposing it with its metaphorical and commercial counterparts. That the CCSS uses these same concepts as metaphors for "text appearance" suggests that it too was influenced by the very sources vilified as not having complexity, nuance, subtlety, depth, or breadth of ideas. By using "light" and "free" as metaphors for "what not to read," these "light" and "free" texts have actually operated in the complex ways text is defined in the CCSS.

## Think of a Look

To put it bluntly, texts, text complexity, and challenging texts now have a "look" (to reference the fashion industry), an appearance to uphold at the expense of twenty-first-century literacies, and have become "America's next top model." That look is the shape of informational texts, specifically argumentative and persuasive texts (Figure 4.2).

If texts are not designed to present information with the complexity outlined in the CCSS, they are considered "light" or "free." Although the CCSS discusses the flexibility that teachers and curriculum developers have in choosing texts, with current legislation that directly aligns teachers' salary with student achievement, there is little doubt that teachers will closely tend to the CCSS "suggested list" of texts, passages, and exercises to ensure that students engage with complex and challenging text. The look of text complexity is written language focused and determined by readability, Lexile scores, inference, multiple plot lines, narrators, nonsequential texts, and cognitive capabilities. By framing text complexity as "trend[ing] downward" with "precipitous declines . . . in average sentence length and vocabulary level in reading textbooks" (National Governors Association 2010, Appendix A, 4), the CCSS incites fear in the public, resulting in assessments that will likely focus on complexity as signaled by Lexile scores (Pearson 2012). The portrait of students who meet the standards will ap-

**Figure 4.2** The Look of Complex Text and Readers: Tagxedo Created from Statements in Appendix A, 24.

pear to have a look of independence, strong content knowledge, and an ability to comprehend and critique written texts—but there will be little to no attention paid to the use of technology and digital media strategically unless it is linked to effective searches for information. They will learn about diversity as it is represented in great classic and contemporary works of literature. Pleasure in reading? Not in the CCSS. I wonder how this "look" will prepare students to work in twenty-first-century classrooms and workspaces when the CCSS values twentieth-century practices?

## THE TWENTY-FIRST-CENTURY LOOK

Contrast the CCSS "look" with that of researchers who study twenty-first-century practices of adolescents and adults, and those who work with digital technologies to design software and hardware that has (and continues to) change how and what we read. Rainie, Zickuhr, Purcell, Madden, and Brenner (2012), researchers for the Pew Internet and American Life Project, found that the number of adult ebook readers quadrupled in the past two years, and those sixteen and older increased from 7 percent to 16–23 percent and read an average of six books per year. Reading print books fell 5 percent (from 72 to 67 percent), statistics that coincide with the increase in ebook reading devices. Twenty-five-year-old multimillionaire

Mike Matas designed and developed a full-length interactive book for the iPad and demonstrated it on the www.ted.com site (one of my favorite "text light" sources), previewing the book experience of the future. *Our Choice* has interactive features that with a touch, tap, swipe, or breath can transform how information is not just read, but experienced. Interestingly, Matas struggled with certain types of writing in high school, and teachers worried that he would not make it in the real world if he could not write. His talents lay in art and design, and he had an intense interest in designing projects, particularly digital texts, through technology. Matas dropped out of high school, developed his own software company, and went on to found Push Pop Press. About his work, Matas states, "My favorite designs are the ones that don't just solve a problem, but also engage you on an emotional level. When there's that balance between functionality and emotion, the two amplify each other and the result is really powerful" (http://whoandwhom.com/mike-matas/). So when CCSS writer David Coleman states, "People really don't give a shit about what you feel or what you think. What they instead care about is can you make an argument with evidence" (see Shannon in this volume), he should talk to directors, designers, engineers, photographers, and others whose work might be categorized as "text light" or "text free."

Books no longer exist on the printed page, and reading is no longer confined to static and print-based texts. I counter Adams' claim that "There may be one day modes and methods of information delivery that are as efficient and powerful as text, but for now there is no contest" (National Governors Association 2010, as cited in Appendix A, 4). That day has come. Twitter, considered a "text light" source by the CCSS, is found to be a "complex phenomenon" by noted researchers Gillen and Merchant (2013, 49). One only has to remember the fatal shooting at Virginia Tech in 2007, where a single gunman killed thirty-three people. The first alert was sent two hours after the first fatal shots were fired. In 2011, again at Virginia Tech, two shooting deaths occurred—but the response time was only seven minutes because of Virginia Tech's use of email, Twitter, and text. The complexity of these tweets, texts, and emails does not lie in CCSS-defined concepts of complexity, but in how these texts moved, morphed, and traversed to thousands of people across geographic boundaries to instantly communicate vital and life-saving information.

# WHOSE TEXT IS IT ANYWAY?

Through use of framing and metaphor, both visual and conceptual constructs, the CCSS has articulated what text means, how complexity is defined in a text, and what constitutes a challenging text. This design is culturally and politically situated by those who believe that learning, knowledge acquisition, and new thought can be gleaned "efficiently" primarily through written language. Education scholar Elliot Eisner (2002) would most likely differ. He writes, "Not everything knowable can be articulated in propositional form. . . . We have a long philosophic tradition in the West that promotes the view that knowing anything requires some formulation of what we know in words; we need to have warrants for our assertions. . . ." And Dewey tells us that while science states meaning, the arts express meaning. Meaning is not limited to what is assertable (12). When the definition of text (and subsequently "text complexity" and "challenging text") is located within the linguistic definition of "a body of writing," an antiquated notion especially in light of twenty-first-century literacy, children's learning will be affected—and not in a good way. Although forty-five states have adopted the CCSS, the design of the standards once adopted will shape learning significantly, again—and not in positive ways.

Now that our world is highly wired and connected and largely multi-mediated, we place importance on students' awareness and understanding of reading and analyzing a range of multimodal texts in order to become critical readers and designers who understand complexity from twenty-first-century perspectives. This entails understanding how texts mean, move, shift, and morph; are remixed, mashed, and transformed; how they act on us, and how we interact with them in ways that position us to take on identities we may wish (or not) to take on (Vasquez, Albers, and Harste 2010). Janks and Vasquez (2011) argue that "the possibilities presented by the new communication landscape, new modes of meaning making, the ongoing transformation of digital texts, the interactivity and immediacy of access . . . continue to provide challenges" (1). However, these challenges and possibilities create spaces for new and exciting opportunities for twenty-first-century students. I agree with Shanahan, Fisher, and Frey's (2012) statement that there is "no more guesswork" (62) in understanding text complexity and challenging texts and the factors that go into it. Unfortunately, that is the problem—they are clearly laid out. If the only way to experience the world and all it has to offer is "through reading great classic and contemporary works of literature," students will continue to tune out of school, keep their heads down, and access digital sources that provide the reading and learning experiences they desire.

# CHAPTER 5

## When Standards Means Standardization

>> MARJORIE FAULSTICH ORELLANA
>> GLORIA-BEATRIZ RODRÍGUEZ

*How do we create spaces for innovation within the Common Core?*

> And the people in the houses
> All went to the university
> Where they were put in boxes
> And they all came out the same
> And there's doctors and lawyers,
> And business executives,
> And they're all made out of ticky tacky
> And they all look just the same.
>
> —Malvina Reynolds

The power of language in poetry and song is revealed in the ways it can move our thinking and inspire contemplation of our values and lived realities. By introducing this essay with the seemingly simple lyrics of Malvina Reynolds' song "Little Boxes," we aim to take up the implicit challenge in Reynolds' words: to consider the "ticky tack" pretense of a system that values only a very narrow kind of success, and that standardizes our thinking so we all look "just the same." In our rapidly transforming world of global migration and transcultural interactions, is "sameness" really a worthy goal? If this is what we want for our children, perhaps the Common Core State Standards

(CCSS) will effect the reproduction of a narrow system of cultural and social values; they may help us to cultivate K–12 students who all look, act, think, read, and write in the same ways.

But we believe most educators do not want this for our students. We believe education is a calling for most who commit to it, and that in our choosing of the profession, we have grappled with complex questions about the goals and purposes of schooling. And as teachers we know, perhaps better than any parent, politician, or technocrat, that each of our students is *unique*. We would surely never want them all to look "just the same." Thus, if our shared goals for education are *not* to "standardize" thinkers, we might question the CCSS and push to implement them in ways that release constraint on innovation, animating and enhancing to the fullest the creative capacities of every child.

In our exploration of standardized learning, we also want to consider whether the pursuit of a common set of standards is likely to level the educational playing field as touted by CCSS proponents. Do we believe it will close the achievement gap between different groups of people and create more "equity" from state to state or school to school? To this end we must consider the *kinds* of literacy practices that are held as the "standard" for all. We do this by analyzing one thread of the CCSS, with an eye to the assumptions embedded within its language. We ask how students who bring diverse, rich, and creative literacy experiences are likely to fare in achieving these measures of success. Our own practices of engaging with dynamic pedagogies that disrupt standardized thinking shed light on the disservice this may do to children, but also *to us all* when we resign ourselves to reproducing the established social order rather than cultivating innovation.

But the CCSS are a de facto new reality, and our intention in offering this critical perspective is not just to stand outside the boxes and point to their ticky-tacky nature. Instead, we want to consider how innovation could be fostered within standards-based education. We will conclude with a discussion of how educators might build from and further cultivate culturally diverse ways of knowing and being, and use those diverse ways to foster innovation for all.

# STANDARD-BEARING AND NORMATIVE PATHWAYS

Language asserts its power to shape our thinking not just in songs and poems, but in the words we choose and the histories embedded in those labels. Foundational to the argument we develop in this essay is exploration of the word "standard," an exercise important to the field as we transition from one "standards" regime to another in 2014. To define education in terms of the achievement of particular "standards" is different than defining it in terms of other kinds of goals, values, or principles. Indeed there are profound (if perhaps-unintended) implications that a standards-based approach may have for what we cultivate (or not) in our students, and for how we set the stage for students to engage with and contribute to our pedagogies. So we begin by examining the meanings that are loaded into the word "standard," considering how the historical origins of the word may unconsciously shape our thinking about teaching and learning when we use the term in the field of education today.

Merriam-Webster's online dictionary defines a *standard* as "something established by authority, custom, or general consent as a model or example." The first definition offered by Merriam-Webster's is "a conspicuous object (as a banner) formerly carried at the top of a pole and used to mark a rallying point especially in battle or to serve as an emblem" (www.merriam webster.com/dictionary/standard). The online etymology dictionary also tells us that the term was used in fourteenth-century France to refer to "units of measures" in weights, and set by the king (the "royal standard") (www .etymonline.com/index.php?term=standard).

From these origins we can perhaps understand our contemporary notion of holding up "high standards" for all, as well as how we use standards as "units of measure" for student learning. But what of these notions of authority, custom, and consent? Whose authority is valued in our standards? Is there general consent as to their validity? From where does that validity stem? And is our notion of standards about rallying troops or groups to move in a single direction? If so, who are the standards bearers who determine what direction that will be?

While studying the children of immigrants who serve as language and culture brokers for their families, Marjorie watched as an eleven-year-old girl tried to explain the construct to her immigrant mother. It wasn't easy. Estela's teacher attempted to parse its meaning by saying "a standard is where we expect kids to be at the end of the year," and Estela provided a fairly literal translation (Orellana 2009). While we can wonder what sense this could have made to her mother, or to Estela herself, more to the point of this essay we might ask: Should the task of teaching involve mapping "where" children "should be" every year? When considering the unique abilities and knowledge possessed by each child, how can we ever determine what *should* be? What happens to students' diverse ways of knowing, being, doing, and thinking, and to the innovation this multiplicity engenders, when we try to define the same normative pathway for all? And when this singular pathway must be traversed to earn a label of "proficient" or "highly proficient," what kinds of kids are likely to fall off or be diverted from that singular pathway? Perhaps more importantly, what other pathways never even get explored?

## LITERACY STANDARDS

The effort to lay out normative pathways to literacy in the CCSS involves first deciding what children should know and be able to do in each grade level in relation to reading and writing. To define this, the standards bearers attempt to break literacy down into its (presumed) component parts, and then to consider how children's understanding of each component "should" develop over time. The conception of literacy embedded in these assumptions could be said to be "autonomous" (Street 2001)—one that defines learning narrowly in relation to the acquisition of particular, predefined skills and content. Autonomists "conceptualise literacy in technical terms, treating it as independent of social context" (Street 2001, 431).

To illustrate, let's look at the "craft and structure" standards for literature, within the language arts, in Grades 1–5—and within these, at the standards that address text structure (one in each grade). By looking across grade levels we get a sense of what the standards bearers believe is important for students to know and do as they presumably grow along "normative" pathways of understanding the structure of different kinds of texts.

In Grade 1 students are expected to "explain major differences between books that tell stories and books that give information, drawing on a wide reading of a range of text types." In Grade 2 they are expected to "describe the overall structure of a story, including describing how the beginning introduces the story and the end concludes the action." In Grade 3 they are expected to "refer to parts of stories, dramas and poems when writing or speaking about a text, using terms such as chapter, scene, and stanza; [and] describe how each successive part builds on earlier sections." In Grade 4 they are to "explain major differences between poems, drama, and prose, and refer to the structural elements of poems (e.g. verse, rhythm, meter) and drama (e.g. casts of characters, settings, descriptions, dialogue, stage directions) when writing or speaking about a text." And in Grade 5 they are expected to "explain how a series of chapters, scenes, or stanzas fits together to provide the overall structure of a particular story, drama or poem."

We do not dispute the value of helping students to analyze the structure of written texts. In many ways these "craft and structure" standards are a considerable improvement over standards that focus attention only on discrete parts of speech or sentence structures. Students are asked to consider the *craft* of stories, and to identify commonalties and divergences in difference structural forms. But can this be done in a way that invites innovation, and that values children's *exploration* of craft and form, rather than leading them down a singular road of "truth"?

The craft and structure standards we outlined above make assumptions about what is emblematic of texts and thus important for children to know. Text structures are treated as clearly differentiated and transparent; each type is presumed to be uniform. It is implied that there are only three important types of texts—poems, drama, and prose—and that these texts have two distinct purposes: either to entertain or to inform (never both, or something else entirely). Poems, drama, and prose each are presumed to have their own structural elements—ones that are taken for granted and presumed obvious. (This is evident in the use of the "e.g."—the adult readers are presumed to know what those structural elements are.) In this strand of the standards, students are not asked to produce these texts as much as to recognize and analyze them.

In contrast to the "autonomous" model of literacy, Street (2001) notes that an "ideological" model of literacy "focuses our attention on the ways in which the apparent neutrality of literacy practices disguises their significance for the distribution of power in society and for authority relations" (Street 2001, 430–31). With this orientation, we might first question whether the things that are presumed to be universal truths about texts are in fact universal. For example, cannot prose be poetic, and enacted as dramas? Perhaps it is a general and universal notion—or at least a starting point—that stories have a beginning, middle, and end, but of course we can imagine stories that are circular, or where action is not neatly concluded at the end. And is it really so transparent a fact that texts serve *either* to inform or entertain? We urge you to jot your own list of the multiplicity of functions that texts have in our lives. Standard schooling narrows these to only two?

For more than thirty years, sociocultural researchers have shown that children from diverse cultural and social class backgrounds have "ways with words" (Heath 1983) that are distinct from those privileged in Western schooling. As an example of how schools can miss the brilliance of our students when they assume there are singular standard literacy practices, James Gee (1985) built on Sarah Michael's (1981) insightful analyses of cultural variations in young children's narrative styles to show how one African American first grader's "share time" story served *both* to inform and entertain. The structure of the child's text, Gee notes, did not follow the implicit normative formula for share time (as a blow-by-blow, short report centered around a particular item or incident); rather the child adopted a formula involving circularity, exaggeration, and poetic redundancy for artistic effect. As a result of this deviation from the informational text structure that the teacher expected (i.e., introduction, development, and resolution), the child's literacy skills were not recognized and she was seen to be "rambling" and "telling lies." Gee shows the reader the artistic skills involved in this child's story/report, and how she builds on a long tradition of oral storytelling in African American communities—a tradition that serves *both* to inform and entertain.

Teachers who understand the importance of building on students' lived experiences will undoubtedly find ways to work with the standards and still build on students' "funds of knowledge" (Moll, Amanti, Neff, and Gonzales 1992). The standards themselves do not *preclude* such pedagogical approaches.[1] But as written, they *do not underscore the importance* of start-ing with what children already know. Nor do they help teachers to recog-nize that children from diverse cultural, social, and linguistic backgrounds may have different ways of structuring or interpreting texts and/or different purposes for engaging with them. The standards also privilege print-based literacies—largely ignoring other oral and visual practices that build on long histories and cultural traditions, and that take on renewed importance in this age of multimodal media.

## WHOSE STANDARDS ARE STANDARD?

So perhaps the problem is less in the idea of *having* a core set of standards than in the content and the ideologies that underlie the standards them-selves. But is it possible to define a set of standards that truly accommo-dates the full range of cultural, linguistic, and imaginative potential of texts (and of children)? Whose standards are assumed to be standard, and whose are likely to be deemed substandard, nonstandard, or other than standard? What other possible "high standards" do we miss when we insist on the same predetermined standards for all?

The CCSS may prove to be just another skewed tool for showing the "de-ficiency" of students who have historically been marginalized by Western schooling practices: African Americans, Latinos, Asian Americans, Native Americans, immigrants, the poor, special education students, and many other kinds of students whose experiences and talents do not map onto a perhaps-mythical cultural norm. Students from the cultural and linguistic traditions that resonate with the standards (i.e., those that presume texts to be easily distinguishable in their purposes, to inform or entertain) may "look smart" when they are asked to describe and analyze school texts because

---

1. The CCSS English Language Arts Standards >> Introduction >> Key Design Consideration Web-page explains that "by emphasizing required achievements, the Standards leave room for teachers, curriculum developers, and states to determine how those goals should be reached. . . . Teachers are thus free to provide students with whatever tools and knowledge their professional judgment and ex-perience identify as most helpful for meeting the goals set out in the standards" (www.corestandards .org/ELA-Literacy/introduction/key-design-consideration).

they have a head start on the epistemological and linguistic foundations for these competencies. But children who have important experiences with other kinds of texts and literacies (e.g., visual, cultural, oral) or with stories or informational texts that do not follow the emblematic norm will be made to look deficient. These same children *will* have a head start on the literacies and practices of their own cultural and linguistic traditions, ones which are not recognized or valued by the standards—nor understood by the standards bearers. But if those competencies are not recognized and built upon, they are in jeopardy of being lost or confused. This strips the child of an opportunity to cultivate her/his unique set of talents, and to see herself/himself as a competent language user. She/he learns what she/he *doesn't* know or *can't* do, and never sees her/his own competencies and potential.

The pursuit of a normative set of standards keeps us from building talents and potentialities that don't fit a rigid, narrow, emblematic norm. This does a disservice to children who have so much to offer and could really flourish if school learning was built on the knowledge and competencies they already possess. This approach does little to "close the achievement gap," a goal articulated by many school reformers.

But it also does a disservice to all of us if our goal is to help our students to think outside the boxes of ticky-tacky that all look just the same. With the standards we place at risk kids' creativity—training them that everything is step-by-step and only one way, that there is one truth rather than different versions or kinds of truth. In so doing we stifle innovation. We also do little to prepare youth to take their place in an increasingly globalized, intercultural, and multimodal world. Stifling innovation may even jeopardize our very futures, because the ability to invent fresh, new ideas is the kind of thinking we will need to ensure our own sustainability on this planet.

## HOW TO BEAR THE STANDARDS?

It is important—indeed, imperative—to step outside the boxes of standards, look at their ticky-tacky nature, and consider other possibilities. At the same time we recognize that the CCSS are a reality, whether we like them or not. Teachers will be expected to be the standards bearers, and to measure students by the "royal standard" units of measure. So before concluding, we want to make a few suggestions for *how* teachers might bear the standards.

First, we should recognize that children bring with them a wide range of language and literacy experiences to school, some of which may be clearly aligned with the standards and some of which may not. We should be very careful as we "measure" children's ability to meet the standards. If some children have a hard time identifying the structure of stories; the difference between fiction and nonfiction; or how to identify the beginning, middle, or end—or to create stories that follow such neat formulas—rather than assume the children are deficient, we might ask what kinds of stories and texts are meaningful in these children's lives. These children may have other understandings of stories and texts; they may have other knowledge that we could learn from. Then, the challenge becomes how to bridge from what kids know to what schools expect of them—how to cultivate children's understanding of "standard" language and literacy practices, forms, and structures; not by conveying that their own language and literacy practices are invalid or insufficient, but by using those very resources as materials for building bridges—in both directions.

We would argue one of the best ways to cultivate an understanding of standard normative frameworks, rules, and structures is to *disrupt* them. As we cultivate students' understanding of the structure of stories, for example, we can try on what it would be like to stop a story in the middle, or to have the ending become the beginning. We can play with the "rules," change things up, and reflect with our students about what happens when we play with structure and form. This can help students to see the underlying rules and structures, but also to see where and how those rules and structures can look different (e.g., in different cultural traditions, or in different genres or media). Ultimately, we can help children to *choose* the forms and structures that work best for them for their own purposes, goals, and aesthetic pursuits—even as they understand the forms that are most recognized and rewarded in the social and academic world.

This is the challenge we would like to leave with our readers. Can we imagine a world in which things are not the way the standards purport them to be? Rather than asserting, "This is the way it is," can we help kids to consider, "How could it be different?" Can we support students as they step outside the boxes to see the ticky-tacky inside, and then to play in a world of possibilities?

# CHAPTER 6

## "Common" and "Core" and the Diversity of Students' Lives and Experiences

>> CATHERINE COMPTON-LILLY

>> KRISTOPHER STEWART

*So how well do the CCSS serve children from diverse backgrounds?*

In the first chapter of her book, *Pathways to the Common Core: Accelerating Achievement*, Lucy Calkins (Calkins, Ehrenworth, and Lehman 2012) highlights some of the potential problems with the Common Core State Standards (CCSS). Among the problems she identifies is the focus on standards rather than poverty and the living situations of families. Specifically, she asks "why is *now* a good time to raise the stakes for our children, when a huge percentage are living in poverty and when the safety nets have been torn apart and there is no funding to improve education?" (3). While Calkins quickly adopts a more optimistic stance, highlighting the potential of the Common Core to accelerate the literacy achievement of students across the United States, her warning haunts us as we consider children we have taught and the historical inequities that have plagued U.S. schools with remarkable consistency.

In this chapter, we take on an issue that intersects with poverty—the challenges children from diverse communities have faced and continue to face with becoming literate. Our major concern rests on the illogical assumption that a "common" and assumedly "core" set of standards could address social inequity and ensure that all children become highly literate. As Berliner and Biddle argued in 1995, various myths about the supposed failure of education in the United States have drawn attention away from what they identify as the real crises in U.S. education—racism and poverty. As they maintain, despite mainstream accounts that blame teachers and cite declining standards, the real problem is our ability to equitably serve the wide range of children who attend U.S. schools. Underfunded schools, limited opportunities for some groups of students, the lack of community resources, and inequitable housing and health care for children contribute significantly to the lowered achievement of children from poor and diverse backgrounds.

The CCSS are based on a backward design model that assumes that a common set of expectations will ensure that all children achieve high outcomes. However, this logic ignores the diversity of experiences and backgrounds that children bring to literacy learning. We raise this point not to make a claim about how much background knowledge children bring to the task of learning to read. Rather, we highlight the remarkable range of ways of being, valuing, knowing, and experiencing that children bring with them as they enter schools. Children have different ways of acting, interacting, and displaying what they know. The historical problem with U.S. schools has been our inability to equitably recognize, value, and build upon these different ways as we plan and implement instruction—and particularly as we assess student progress (Willis 2008).

In this chapter, we offer a brief but close analysis of the CCSS in an attempt to identify to what extent student diversity is recognized and addressed. We then explore a critical dimension of the Common Core, the idea that meaning resides with texts and the concurrent implication that experiences from students' lives, including diverse ways of making sense, are undervalued and ultimately considered to lead to inaccurate readings (Calkins, Ehrenworth, and Lehman 2012). We open the conversation by positing what we mean by "diverse students" and highlighting why diversity matters as children become readers and writers.

## STUDENT DIVERSITY AND WHY IT MATTERS

*Diversity* is essentially a problematic term. When white people use the term diversity, they inherently imply that others, people who are not white, are diverse. While recognizing the dangers that inescapably accompany the term, we use *diversity* to refer to all of the dimensions of being human that accompany and explain the differential experiences, opportunities, privileges, and situations that people encounter as they move through school and their lives. Diversity can reflect race, culture, social class, language practices, gender, religion, appearance, sexuality, and a range of other dimensions. In relation to the argument that we present on these pages, diversity is also any aspect of self and/or community that has historically affected people and continues to differentially limit opportunities, allow privileges, and impose inequity. We recognize diversity with the understanding that schools, as well as other social institutions, operate with regimes of power that generally reward particular ways of being while failing to recognize and value others.

This is why diversity matters in schools and classrooms. Diversity means that children bring various "funds of knowledge" (Gonzalez, Moll, and Amanti 2005) to classrooms and educators must consciously and consistently work to identify and build upon these rich bodies of knowledge. As revealed in the following section, attending to the diversity of students' backgrounds is difficult when a "common" set of "core" standards neither recognizes nor reflects the multiple ways of being, knowing, and thinking that children bring to classrooms. In other words, by privileging one way of being literate and making sense of texts, the Common Core limits what counts for students who bring different ways of acting, interacting, and displaying what they know.

## A BRIEF ANALYSIS OF THE CCSS

While a thorough review of the CCSS is impossible within this single chapter, we believe that this brief but detailed analysis will provide readers with a sense of the issues that accompany the use of this common set of standards with children who bring diverse experiences and perspectives to literacy classrooms. In short, the examples offered below should be treated as representative of the tone and content of the complete document. Due to limitations of space, we limit ourselves to an analysis of the "K–5 Reading, College and Career Readiness Anchor Standards for Reading" (Common Core State Standards 2010, 36–43) and highlight three discernable, and potentially problematic, patterns within these standards: (1) a focus on recounting, retelling, and summarizing, (2) a focus on text structure and organization, and (3) reading as a process of discerning correct meanings directly from texts.

## A Focus on Recounting, Retelling, and Summarizing

The CCSS highlight four main areas: key ideas and details, craft and structure, integration of knowledge and ideas, and range of reading and text complexity. Within the section dedicated to "key ideas and details" is a set of standards that highlight recounting, retelling, and summarizing. Below I offer quotes from these standards to illustrate the expectations placed on students as they read both literature and informational text.

When working with literature, children are expected to:

> With prompting and support, *retell* familiar stories, including key details. (Kindergarten; Standard #2, 37)

> *Recount* stories, including fables and folktales from diverse cultures, and determine their central message, lesson, or moral. (Grade 2; Standard #2, 37)

> *Determine the theme* of a story, drama, or poem from details in the text . . . *summarize* the text. (Grade 5; Standard #2, 38)

Concurrently, when working with informational texts, children are expected to:

> With prompting and support, identify the main idea and *retell key details* of a text. (Kindergarten; Standard #2, 39)

> Determine the main idea of a text; *recount the key details* and explain how they support the main idea. (Grade 3; Standard #2, 40)

> Determine two or more main ideas of a text and explain how they are supported by key details; *summarize the text.* (Grade 5; Standard #2, 40)

Several points are significant. First, recounting, retelling, and summarizing are fairly low-level skills. They entail holding information from the text in one's mind and reproducing it for an audience. These tasks entail neither analysis nor evaluation of the texts. Instead, they entail a literal recount of what was read, requiring the reader to focus on the text as a stand-alone entity unconnected to the reader, her/his experiences, and the reader's world beyond the text.

### A Focus on Text Structure and Organization

Recognize *common types of texts*. (Kindergarten; Standard #5, 37)

Describe the *overall structure* of a story. (Grade 2; Standard #5, 37)

Explain how a series of chapters, scenes, or stanzas fits together to provide the *overall structure* of a particular story, drama, or poem. (Grade 5; Standard #5, 38)

The quotes from the CCSS presented above were all taken from standards related to craft and structure that reference literature. A parallel set of standards, focused on structure, are provided for informational texts:

*Know and use various text features* (e.g., headings, table of contents, glossaries, electronic menus, icons) to locate key facts or information in a text. (Grade 1; Standard #5, 39)

*Describe the overall structure* (e.g., chronology, comparison, cause/effect, problem/solution) of events, ideas, concepts or information in a text or part of a text. (Grade 4; Standard #5, 40)

Together, these standards illustrate a focus on the internal structures of texts and the ways stories and informational texts are presented. Mastering these standards requires children to analyze the texts they encounter without attending explicitly to the content of those texts or to information beyond the texts. The focus is on craft without involving the ways of being, valuing, knowing, and experiencing that children bring to texts. Inherently, children must treat the text as the object of analysis, dismissing content and their possible responses to the content presented. Thus a child reading commonly used texts such as *The Snowy Day* (Keats 1962) would not be expected to comment on Peter's race and the same child reading a book by Judy Blume would not be expected to notice the absence of substantive African American characters. This might seem insignificant, and one could argue that focusing on text structure is sufficient. However, children bring different questions and reactions to texts and take up the messages inherent in texts differently. In addition, cultural groups have different ways of structuring and telling stories that are worthy of attention and consideration. CCSS that focus on text structures, as well as those addressing other aspects of texts, almost exclusively limit analyses to what is presented in texts, silencing insights that reflect the diversity of children's experiences and knowledge.

### Reading as a Process of Discerning Correct Meanings Directly from Texts

While the title of the section of the standards dedicated to the "integration of knowledge and ideas" might suggest that children are expected to connect texts to their own lives, the content of these standards paints a very different picture. In short, these standards focus on the integration of knowledge and ideas within particular texts or—in cases of Grades 3, 4, and 5—across small sets of texts.

In the standards for literature, kindergarten students who read literature texts "with prompting" are expected to "describe the *relationship between illustrations and the story* in which they appear" (Common Core State Standards 2010, 37) while fifth grade students, also reading literature, must "analyze how visual and multimedia events *contribute to the meaning*, tone, or beauty of a text" (38). While the fifth grade standard presents a multimodal definition of text that includes graphic novels and multimedia presentations, the standards' focus remains on the internal consistency of these texts. Standards for informational texts are similar with first grade students using "illustrations and details in a text to *describe its key elements*" (39) and fourth grade students interpreting "information presented visually or quantitatively (e.g., in charts, graphs, diagrams, timelines, animations, or interactive elements on Web pages)" and explaining "how the information *contributes to an understanding* of the text in which it appears" (40).

While some of the standards presented under the heading of "integration of knowledge and ideas" do invite students to "compare and contrast stories" (Grade 5, 38) "draw on multiple print or digital sources" (Grade 5, 40), and "integrate information from several texts" (Grade 5, 40), these standards require students to construct meaning through the analysis of multiple teacher-provided texts rather than inviting students to draw on their own experiences and cultural knowledge. Meaning is situated within texts, rather than within students and communities. In its most blatant and perhaps extreme inculcation, one might ask what this means to a Puerto Rican child who is reading an account of the voyage of Columbus that does not acknowledge the violence inflicted on the Taíno people or an African American student who encounters a reference to Malcolm X in a textbook that does not recognize his role as a human rights activist. Textual meaning does not reside solely in texts; meaning is a human construction that always involves multiple ways of being, knowing, and thinking—and human experiences beyond any particular text.

Together the standards cited above privilege the literal meanings found in texts, focus on analyses of text structures, and view reading as a process of ascertaining the author's intended, and perhaps singular, meaning. The diverse backgrounds of students are neither acknowledged nor accessed. While on the surface this may appear to treat reading and making sense of texts as neutral—and thus unaffected by students' experiences, cultures, and ways of being—in actuality this perpetuates the status quo, the privileging of particular ways of making sense of texts, and the reification of existing criteria for evaluating students.

## THE COMMON CORE AND MEANING CONSTRUCTION

As Calkins, Ehrenworth, and Lehman (2012) note, there are several things that the Common Core does not do. In particular, they argue that the Common Core does not ask students to "make text-to-self connections, access prior knowledge, explore personal response, and relate to your own life" (25). In short, they maintain that the Common Core "de-emphasizes reading as a personal act and emphasizes textual analysis" (35). Calkins explicitly connects these practices to the "New Criticism" approach to reading and textual analysis that originated in the 1930s and 1940s and dominated instruction in college and high school English classrooms in the 1950s (Willinsky 1990). The New Critics promoted the close reading of the text, arguing that text structures contributed to textual meaning while maintaining that personal perspectives distracted readers from ascertaining the true meanings of texts. Four decades ago, Rosenblatt (1978/1994) and others challenged these notions by redefining reading as a transactional process involving both texts and readers.

While the type of textual analysis promoted by the New Critics and the CCSS might be one way of analyzing texts, it is a particularly dangerous approach when working with students who may find the literal meanings of texts limited, incomplete, and often dismissive of their own knowledge and experiences. Beach, Thein, and Webb (2012) note that much of the resistance to the bureaucratic imposition of the CCSS has come from "teachers who value a bottom-up focus on their own unique, local school cultural contexts and particular students' needs, interests, and knowledge" (10). They argue that the CCSS fail to acknowledge cultural diversity and worry that assessments that accompany the Common Core, like literacy assessments of the past (Willis 2008), will continue to privilege students who bring particular types of knowledge and capital while failing to "recognize the cultural diversity of America's student population" (Beach, Thein, and Webb 2012, 13).

Based on this dismissal of the views and perspectives of students from diverse backgrounds, Beach and his colleagues (2012) point to a fundamental problem with the CCSS—their inability to address achievement gaps related to poverty and race. They cite the need for increased resources to underfunded schools and to communities—including support for equitable employment opportunities, housing, wages, and health care. Beach (2011) argues that cognitive and formalist assumptions that shape the CCSS and the assessments that are being developed to assess students' progress toward these standards will be particularly detrimental to "low-income students of color who lack access to linguistic or cultural capital" (25).

Since the CCSS do not directly address the social inequities inherent in our classrooms, it is imperative that teachers and administrators realize that the standards are woefully inadequate in seizing upon the diverse lived experiences students bring with them. Instead of forcing students to engage only with texts, teachers must encourage students to also engage with each other in order to promote diversity, critical thinking, and personal agency.

Assuming that the real problems in American education lie with the achievement gap that separates white, middle class students from students who bring diverse cultures and social class experiences to classrooms

(Berliner and Biddle 1995), it seems unlikely that a "common" and "core" curriculum will be the key to serving diverse students who bring varied cultural knowledge, socioeconomic experiences, language practices, gender positionings, religions, physical appearances, and sexual orientations to classrooms. In short, the knowledge and experiences of too many students could be left behind, highlighting the potential of the CCSS to exacerbate rather than address inequity.

# CHAPTER 7

## *All I'm Asking for Is . . .*

>> S A N D R A   W I L D E

**What you want?**

When I started researching documents and examples of Common Core State Standards (CCSS) professional development for teachers, I felt like I was in a garden of forking paths or a *Choose Your Own Adventure* book. A Google search for "Common Core State Standards professional development" had more than four million hits, the first page alone including links to professional organizations, state departments of education, school districts, and organizations whose provenance was unclear. Every site led to multiple other sites.

Although my first response was that there are a lot of resources out there, my second thought was that there must be a lot of money out there, creating markets for professional development providers. My immediate concern was that I could spend a year just exploring what kinds of professional development were being offered or mandated, who was going to be providing them, and what they might entail. However, I reminded myself quickly that I'd agreed to write a chapter about how teachers were represented in, by, and for the Common Core, and that investigation seemed too far from the living, breathing human beings in classrooms with students.

I decided, therefore, to choose my own adventure, first by following an online trail through some of the major players in CCSS professional development—with examples of what's being proposed from the state level down to the lesson-plan level, focusing particularly on where teachers are expected to fit into official plans. This adventure felt too big still—so I fixed my gaze on text complexity aspects of CCSS-sponsored professional development. These aspects are expected to be new and challenging for teachers and English language arts teaching, and therefore afford me a good vantage point to see how teachers are officially positioned in bringing the Common Core to students. After my analysis of a few examples, however, I decided to conclude this chapter by comparing and contrasting that position with those offered to teachers in professional development projects I've been involved in over the last few decades.

## CCSS PROFESSIONAL DEVELOPMENT

I began my analysis with a statement from Chapter 6 of *Implementing Common Core State Standards and Assessments: A Workbook for State and District Leaders*, developed for the Partnership for Assessment of Readiness for College and Careers (PARCC) assessment consortium by Achieve and the U.S. Education Delivery Institute.

> Professional development—defined as the time and money diverted to increasing the knowledge and skills of teachers and school leaders—can be a powerful mechanism to improve instructional practice. State and district leaders recognize that massive and widespread efforts are needed to provide highly effective and cost-efficient professional development on the CCSS. (www.achieve.org/files/Common_Core_Workbook.pdf, 6.3)

In Chapter 6, professional development becomes an economic decision about how resources will be allocated in bringing the Common Core to classroom practice. Given the source of this statement, this definition seems official. Achieve is the agency that the National Governors Association, philanthropic foundations, and corporations formed in 1996 to broker rigorous state academic standards. The U.S. Education Delivery Institute is an import from Great Britain's education reform during the first decade of the twenty-first-century, carrying the concept of "delivery" to America—"a systematic process through which public sector leaders can drive progress and deliver results" (www.deliveryinstitute.org/delivery-approach). PARCC is a twenty-two-state consortium working together to develop next-generation K–12 assessments for English language arts (see Chapter 9 for more on PARCC). This definition and process, of course, focus on professional development from the high end of the food chain—state and local administrators who are "diverting" resources from other areas of school budgets in order to improve teacher practice, with an assumption that the planning for it will come from the top down.

What struck me about this document is the extent to which it defines professional development as a bureaucratic process. Chapter 6 reproduces a "delivery chain" for one exemplar state that includes (in descending order of authority) the state commissioner; a state curriculum and instruction team; a regional committee; content provider organizations and instructors chosen at the state and regional level; district curriculum directors; school principals, coaches, and professional learning community facilitators; classroom teachers; and students. Attention is given to monitoring coherence throughout the professional development chain. Included in the twenty-page chapter are forms for establishing and maintaining measures of success: alignment to the state's model; user (principal and teacher) satisfaction; classroom practice (via self-report or observation); and impact on student outcomes. The decisions about which professional development providers to hire are reserved for state and regional officials, although their impact will be monitored locally.

I followed links from Chapter 6 to classroom resources in order to identify an expected disposition for teachers near the end of the chain. This action led me to professional development models from Achieve the Core (www.achievethecore.org/steal-these-tools/professional-development-modules). A module called "Introduction to the ELA/Literacy Shifts" provides Power-Point slides naming the three major shifts in literacy curriculum required for CCSS, including a section on expected regular practice with complex text and its academic language. The slides are intended to reorient teachers from pursuing NCLB state standards to delivering the Common Core. In broad strokes, they present three big ideas: too many students are reading at too low a level; students should be reading increasingly complex text as they progress through grades K–12; and students should have their reading scaffolded through multiple readings, read-aloud, chunking text, and close analytic reading. On the slides, the transition is treated as fact, leaving little room for teachers to ask basic questions about the need for the transition or the reorientation. Reading through the slides, I realized that the delivery chain establishes a chain of command as well as one of logistics.

I backtracked to the PARCC website in order to locate professional development videos and lesson plans. PARCC has links to a number of teaching videos, but I wanted something clearly identified as "this is what we mean with the standards, and here's how to do it," so I chose a video featuring David Coleman (who is often referred to as the architect of the CCSS) teaching a lesson on Martin Luther King Jr.'s "Letter from a Birmingham Jail." This video is available on YouTube, and many state Department of Education websites link to it. (Both the video and transcript can be found in Part 6 of http://usny.nysed.gov/rttt/resources/bringing-the-common-core-to-life-download.html.) Note that Coleman was speaking to an audience of educators, not K–12 students, and therefore he was both modeling teaching and talking about pedagogy and curriculum.

The lesson is meant to be a brief introduction to a recommended six to eleven days of teaching at the high school level about King's seven-thousand-word document (available at http://www.africa.upenn.edu/Articles_Gen/Letter_Birmingham.html). The lesson was an early example (presented in April of 2011) of close reading as a model for helping students to read complex text. Speaking to the teachers, Coleman is explicitly critical of typically recommended before-reading activities, such as providing students with background knowledge, because he understands the practice as failing to engage students with the text itself. (See Chapter 3 for more on Coleman's understanding.) His demonstration begins by reading aloud the first paragraph of King's letter and asking questions about the text itself (note that this is a verbatim transcript rather than a polished edited copy of his remarks).

> I want to say perhaps the first question you might ask about this text is, "Based on this text and this text alone, what do you know? What can you make out about the letter King received?" So let's

look again at that first paragraph for a moment and we might make out gradually that they've accused him of saying very specific [sic], of being unwise and untimely. We're going to go back to that first question. A clever student might notice that he wrote to his dear fellow clergymen, which reveals something about who wrote the letter and perhaps something about King himself if they understand the construct "fellow clergymen" which you might work on with them immediately or it will actually come up later. But we can already know at least two things, it's written from clergymen and says you've been unwise and untimely.

(New York State Department of Education, 2011)

Coleman continues with a discussion of King's rhetorical strategies in his next few paragraphs of the letter, particularly the arguments King uses to make his case for coming as an outsider to participate in protests in Birmingham. Coleman is clearly making an argument himself in modeling this lesson, an argument that complex text can best be approached through teacher-guided close reading, walking students through the text in great detail. His video is about twenty-five minutes long, but the lessons on digging within the four corners of King's letter and commenting on its vocabulary are expected to last for a week or two.

After I chose this video, I discovered online that it has received much attention not just as a good example, but as a highly circulated virtual mandate of what teachers' practice should look like. Although CCSS officials argue that they don't mandate teaching methodology, this type of video professional development sends a strong message about instructional methods. And the guide to publishers concerning the close reading anchor standard explains that such reading "often requires compact, short, self-contained texts that students can read and re-read deliberately and slowly to probe and ponder the meanings of individual words, the order in which sentences unfold, and the development of ideas over the course of the text." (See Chapter 7 for more on the CCSS guide for publishers.) The Coleman video describes and demonstrates how this should play out between a teacher and older readers.

Close reading isn't just for high school students. The Achieve the Core website (2012) has multiple lessons for close reading at a variety of grade levels. These are in a section called "Steal These Tools," clearly intended for teachers to use directly for their own professional development. I examined "The Fisherman and His Wife" for third grade, which provides five days of lessons for this familiar Grimm Brothers folktale (2,400 words long in this version). The lessons are reminiscent of basal reader teachers' manuals, with perhaps greater attention to examining the text itself, such as looking for examples of how and why the sea changes throughout the story (hint—it's as the wishes get more extravagant and the fish gets increasingly angry); this is the big idea that is expected to take up four days of instruction. I can't resist quoting two bad examples of Achieve the Core teaching ideas focusing on the language of the text. Remember these are intended for eight- and nine-year-old students.

1. Playing with Words
   "O man, O man!—if man you be,
   Or flounder, flounder, in the sea—
   Such a tiresome wife I've got,
   For she wants what I do not."
   —from *The Fisherman and His Wife*

Use the template below to rewrite this verse as if you were the Fisherman talking to a female tuna fish. Then think of another word to describe your wife.
   "O _____, O _____!—if _____ you be,
   Or _____, _____, in the sea—
   Such a(n) _____ wife I've got,
   For she wants what I do not."

2. We write differently than we speak. The language in this story is more formal than the language you might use when talking to your friends. Here is a simple trick you can use to "translate" some of the sentences so that they sound more familiar and are easier to understand.

Directions: Read each sentence from the story out loud. Then, replace the underlined words with a contraction. Read the new sentence out loud.

Example:

Sentence from the story: "Look," said the wife, "is not that nice?"
New sentence: "Look," said the wife, "isn't that nice?" (2012)

(This is, of course, archaic rather than contemporary formal language that is being made less formal.)

CCSS officials offer public school teachers several positions. Good teachers are lauded as the solution to the United States' problems, helping students to mine information from texts in order to make arguments based on textual warrants, and therefore preparing them for careers or college. But teachers must earn the "good" designation by renouncing some of the previous best practices of engaging students' prior knowledge before reading and encouraging them to make text-to-self and text-to-world connections. To become reeducated about reading and how to teach it, and texts and how to use them, CCSS offer teachers positions at the end of the professional development delivery chain where they are to accept decisions made at higher levels of authority, and then enact them by following along with the models and materials provided for them. CCSS professional development, then, positions teachers as consumers of ideas, practices, and commodities in order to earn the designation of "good teacher" by filing self-reports of compliance, inviting observation according to delivery plans, and producing students with high scores on new assessments. The words "professional" and "development" are subverted in the official CCSS bureaucratic system and could be replaced with more accurate descriptors—technician and training.

## A LITTLE RESPECT

It doesn't have to be this way. What if we assumed that teachers are smart and interested in their work, capable of thinking deeply about the challenges of helping all students negotiate their current circumstances as well as preparing them for what could be their futures? What if, instead of placing teachers at the end of the delivery chain, school reform placed them in positions in which they could name the problems, develop alternative routes toward solutions, test them in their classrooms, and talk about their successes and struggles with their peers—not just follow the signs that someone with more authority (but less experience) has posted? These assumptions and ideas are as old as Dewey's pragmatism for teachers (1899) and as new as collaborative teacher inquiry (Cochran-Smith & Lytle 2009). And they are embraced by professional organizations like the National Council of Teachers of English (2006). What might this look like?

First, teachers working together without intimidation would address the problematic content, texts, and procedures that CCSS officials think are good for them. Consider Coleman's lesson on "Letter from a Birmingham Jail." Coleman misstates some facts. The clergymen that King is responding to didn't write him a letter, they wrote a statement that was published in the local newspaper. King didn't see the statement until he'd been in jail for two days and a colleague brought it to him. The clergyman were white (and yes, their race matters) "moderates" who were making part of a case common in 1963—that the civil rights movement's goals were laudable (which was hard for even moderates to deny at the time), but that it was trying to move too fast. The criticisms of outsiders participating in demonstrations were part of a stalling tactic; the somewhat rapid changes in civil rights law and policy that eventually came about were in large part because of President Kennedy's assassination and President Johnson's successful enactment of civil rights legislation as part of Kennedy's legacy.

Coleman doesn't mention the circumstances of the composition of King's letter. His jailers didn't provide him with paper; King wrote furiously in the margins of the newspaper his colleague had given him and on other scraps of paper, including toilet paper, and had his associates carry these pieces outside of the jail. It went through a long editing process before it was published as an open letter. It was never actually put in envelopes and mailed to the white clergymen (information about this history comes from Frady 2005).

Teachers know that content and context matter. History teachers considering teaching from this text would surely recognize that students can't understand King's message without an accurate understanding of the facts surrounding its production and distribution, and English teachers would recognize the need to push beyond the boundaries of the four corners of the letter itself to understand what it means (not just its meaning). King's intent, even in this single context, means more than his words (powerful as they might be) convey. Good teachers, thinking teachers, know this from their everyday work with readers.

The trouble with the "Fisherman and his Wife" lesson begins with the choice of this text. The creator of the lesson plans, whose name is not given, chose an 1886 translation from the German. Like many of the CCSS exemplar texts, this text was almost certainly selected because it's no longer in copyright and can be reproduced without permission or expense. A contemporary picture book version (Isadora 2008) is thirty-two pages long, with lively collage illustrations set in an African landscape. The plot of both versions is a basic folktale story about excessive wishes to a supernatural power leaving the demander with nothing—something easily understood by young children. Teachers thinking about text complexity would ask what is this text, an old or new version, doing in a third-grade lesson? Its plot is too simple. Moreover, the contemporary version eliminates any need for the dreadful language activities assigned apparently to keep the single text in play for a week of instruction and to help students deal with the archaic language of the old translation.

Second, teachers in charge of their professional development would find that we know quite a bit about helping students attempt more challenging texts. For example, we know that children start with easy books and then move into harder ones, and that the reading itself, along with appropriate scaffolding from the teacher, helps them learn how to read the harder books. One important role for teachers is connecting students with books that are "just right" for them and also those that are a bit of a stretch (Calkins et al. 2012), and providing a classroom climate that encourages reading—including having plenty of books available. Few good teachers would advocate addressing the problem of students reading too many simple texts by dragging students through books that are too hard for them, and that need a great deal of teacher guidance for students to make sense of, just because those books are what they "should" be reading at their grade level. Teachers in charge of their own professional development can spend an hour with a good children's librarian to develop a good list of books that would be a "stretch" books for their students.

Useful professional development to increase text complexity might involve school-based teams' thinking about what their students are reading, how to help them set reading goals for themselves, how to stretch into books that are a little bit harder, and so on. They could bring in fresh alternatives on the topic through reading and discussing some of the many professional books that are being published on teaching with the standards and existing books about children's literature; finding online resources to read, watch, and discuss; attending professional conferences together; and so on. They may not need official "providers" at all, and certainly should be free to select their own if they do. How could district- and regional-level administrators choose wisely among providers of "deliverables" when the examples provided in the belly of the beast are so problematic?

Third, after the problem is identified and viable alternatives are vetted through careful study, then teachers in charge of their professional development would test the practices they think most viable in their classrooms. Here the complexities of complexity would be revealed in the lives of teachers and students in real, not imagined, classrooms (see Chapters 5 and 6 about diversity). A single text and the Socratic method (Coleman's choices) could work for some, but would not afford all students ways to act on engaging complex texts. Rather the curriculum and pedagogy—even the texts—would need to allow multiple points of entry if all students were to profit from the new alternative practice (see Chapter 3 for more about text). The complexities of complexity would require the teachers in charge of professional development to develop more subtle formative assessments of movement toward and success in reading challenging texts. The new CCSS tests, even when mediated through computer screens, will be too slow and too blunt to enable teachers to make meaningful decisions about how to help students in their classrooms.

Although the official CCSS statements about professional development and the tools they offer to develop teachers' capacity warrant the conclusion that CCSS officials view teachers as consumers, and not producers, of curriculum and pedagogy, they do state at the end of the "Myths and Facts" webpage:

The best understanding of what works in classrooms comes from the teachers who are in them. That's why these standards will establish *what* students need to learn, but they will not dictate *how* teachers should teach. Instead, schools and teachers will decide how best to help students reach the standards. (www.corestandards.org/about-the-standards/myths-vs-facts)

Teachers should insist that this statement be the first slide in every school's professional development project. At the very least, it mouths the sentiment of respect. Teachers in charge of their professional development can sing it loud.

# CHAPTER 8

## Jack and Miss Stretchberry Meet the Common Core: And What Lessons Do They Find There?

>> ELIZABETH JAEGER

*What lessons do they find there?*

Standards are the adopted "what" of instruction. Curriculum is the enacted "how." The question that shapes this chapter is how instructional materials (and the people who fund and publish them) will mediate the spaces in between those points. When teachers and administrators go to the marketplace in search of these materials, what will they find?

## LOVE THAT DOG . . . LOVE THAT POEM

But first, a brief step back in time. It was nearly twenty-five years into my career as an educator before I worked up the gumption to teach poetry in my classroom. I certainly enjoyed the genre; reading poetry aloud was a treasured, if relatively infrequent, pastime. But attempt to convey to children that the writing and sharing of poetry was both magical and sweet? This seemed well beyond my capabilities.

Then two things happened. First, in an effort to polish my writing workshop protocol, I registered for a seminar given by Nancie Atwell. One of the major takeaways from that day was that experiences with poetry fundamentally alter children as authors. They acquire the language and thought processes of poets largely by osmosis and those acquisitions carry over into whatever writing they do hence—from personal narrative to persuasive essay to expository report. Teach poetry first, Atwell argued, and your students will reap the benefits all year long. "But how?" I thought. Atwell, to her credit, is not one to script the teaching of writing.

And then I stumbled upon *Love That Dog*, a children's book by Sharon Creech. Miss Stretchberry, a grade school teacher attempting to teach poetry, encounters Jack, a student who must be convinced that this is a worthy endeavor. However, even his initial outright refusal takes the form of a poem-of-sorts:

> I don't want to
> because boys
> don't write poetry.
> Girls do. (2001, 1)

Creech chronicles Jack's exposure to a range of poetry—from Robert Frost to William Blake to Walter Dean Myers—and the ways it feeds his poetic efforts. While never stated, it seems that Miss Stretchberry is reading poems aloud in class, allowing the children to soak up structure and language, tone and timbre. After hearing William Carlos Williams' poem "The Red Wheelbarrow," Jack timidly offers what he believes to be his first verse:

> Do you promise
> not to read it
> out loud?
> Do you promise
> not to put it
> on the board?
> Okay, here it is,
> but I don't like it.
>
>> *So much depends*
>> *upon*
>> *a blue car*
>> *splattered with mud*
>> *speeding down the road.* (2001, 4)

Could I do this? Could I share with my students poetry that moved me and expect that they would respond as Jack had done? In the weeks that followed, I read aloud to them, they read aloud to me and to their friends (each in her/his own voice), and they wrote, using the poems we read as models—or not. That was the curriculum.

## THE STANDARDS AND THE MARKETPLACE

What does this tale have to do with the Common Core State Standards (CCSS) and with instructional materials produced, distributed, and consumed in service of those standards? In short, Jack and Miss Stretchberry have wandered into published curriculum designed to address the Common Core. But before we follow that story, let's take a quick look at some of the standards-based curriculum products that are currently (or soon to be) available.

The authors of the Common Core argue that, while the standards (the *what* of education) were initiated by those outside the classroom, it will be the responsibility of teachers to craft instruction (the *with what tools* and *in what way* elements of education). There is tension here, however, because these same initiators have produced recommended reading lists (Common Core State Standards in the English Language Arts and Literacy: List of Text Exemplars 2012), which may become *the tools*, and the *Revised Publisher's Criteria for the Common Core State Standards* (Coleman and Pimentel 2012a, 2012b), which may become *the way*. At this point, it is uncertain just how influential these documents will prove to be. For this reason, I'll briefly review a range of CCSS products that fall at various points along a continuum from less to more prescriptive and from less to more concerned with harnessing market forces on their behalf.

Heinemann authors and reading/writing workshop advocates Lucy Calkins, Mary Ehrenworth, and Christopher Lehman (2012) have written a largely descriptive book called *Pathways to the Common Core: Accelerating Achievement*. Early on, the authors hint at ambivalence—beginning with their concerns about who developed the standards adopted by states, how more recent documents have served to rigidify implementation of the standards, and (most significantly) about the inadequate view of reading these documents espouse. But by page seven, the authors have made a conscious decision to view the CCSS as "gold," and to—somehow—employ them in service of their own agenda.[1] With chapter titles such as "Overview of the Reading Standards: What Do They Say and What Does This Mean for Us?" it is clear that these authors will not tell teachers what to do, but rather help to clarify the intent of the standards and how they are likely to influence instructional mandates.[2]

A second set of instructional materials dispenses with philosophical discussions about the standards but also avoids prescribing specifically what teachers are to do. One might refer to this type of publication as a *framework*, exemplified by Owocki's (2012) *Common Core Lesson Book, K–5: Working with Increasingly Complex Literature, Informational Text, and Foundational Reading Skills*. The book is organized into the three sections noted in the title and, within each section, by anchor standard. What the book does *not* do is to prescribe how the standards should be taught at particular grade levels (although some hints are provided), nor does it specify particular texts to be used for this purpose.

While the titles noted above are relatively nonprescriptive, it has been my experience that if there exists an opportunity to tell teachers exactly what to do and how and when to do it—and to make money off doing so—there will be no shortage of entities ready to take advantage of that opportunity; the CCSS movement has proven to be no exception. There are several major online efforts to provide complete lesson plans that address particular standards. The lessons are prescriptive, but they do not comprise a comprehensive curriculum. I'll look at two of the online efforts: LearnZillion and Share My Lesson.

In a webinar broadcast on November 1, 2012, LearnZillion cofounder Eric Westendorf described the handpicked teachers responsible for developing the lessons available on the LearnZillion website as the Dream Team.

---

1. This may be why Kathleen Porter-Magee (2012) of the Fordham Institute has accused these authors of promoting a "damaging misdirection of the expectations laid out in the Common Core standards."

2. While their materials are just beginning to emerge, the International Reading Association and the NCTE seem to be taking a similar approach (e.g., *The Common Core: Teaching K–5 Students to Meet the Reading Standards* [McLaughlin and Overturf 2012]; *Supporting Students in a Time of Core Standards* [Williams, Homan, and Swofford 2011]).

Westendorf goes on to note that these teachers were paid by the Bill and Melinda Gates Foundation.[3] The goal here is to provide over two thousand lessons linked to the CCSS. However, LearnZillion's lessons are essentially unrelated to the basic mission of the standards. When individual states developed their own English language arts standards in the 1980s and 1990s, they tended to reflect the National Reading Panel's emphasis on decoding and fluency. However, the CCSS relegate these so-called "foundational skills" to the end of the document and emphasize close reading, managing text complexity, and producing clear arguments. In contrast, LearnZillion's lessons for third graders include twenty lessons facilitating close reading, eight scaffolding text complexity, and not a single lesson dealing with argumentation. There are a full seventy-eight lessons designed to promote accurate and fluent reading.

The Share My Lesson website is a sort of electronic bulletin board "by teachers, for teachers"—a joint enterprise of the American Federation of Teachers and Think, Educate, Share its counterpart in the United Kingdom. It is, as Ohanian (2012) puts it, a "free-for-all jumble; if there is any vetting, it isn't apparent." Here there are 380 lessons listed in the foundational skills section at the third-grade level, but they range from letter sounds to reading comprehension in no apparent order. Even assuming that the lessons are of high quality, it is unlikely that a teacher could efficiently find what she/he needed on this site.

As might be expected, the major textbook publishers are entering the CCSS market with new core literacy programs. Unlike LearnZillion and Share My Lesson, these programs purport to be completely comprehensive. McGraw-Hill Education is among the largest publishers of K–12 reading materials (McGraw-Hill Education 2012) and its flagship product, *Open Court Reading*, was the most commonly adopted curriculum purchased with Reading First funding (Borman, Dowling, and Schneck 2008). Of their latest major endeavor, *Reading Wonders*, McGraw-Hill states that it is the "first K–6 reading program built specifically for the Common Core" (McGraw-Hill Education 2013). While the product is in its pilot phase (and requests to the

---

3. The Gates Foundation has provided financial support for a number of products described in this chapter, including Share My Lesson and the *Common Core Curriculum Maps* project.

director of media relations to preview the materials were unsuccessful), we learn three major things from the official press release:

- The program is designed to prepare students for the 2014–2015 CCSS assessments.
- It is based on the *Revised Publisher's Criteria*.
- It emphasizes "close reading" (McGraw-Hill Education 2013)

When we put the term *Reading Wonders* into an Internet search engine, the most accessible information is a video story including characters from the text produced by the animation studio Nathan Love (also responsible for ad campaigns designed to sell Goldfish™ Sandwich Bread and Sweet'n Low, among other products). A gold key passes from one character to another— a crab, a chipmunk, and a polar bear dressed as an astronaut—until it is finally employed to ignite a rocket ship that takes the characters to . . . a place where animals closely read nonfiction texts in search of evidence to support argumentative writing. This product is slated for general release in 2014.

Of the products I reviewed, which offers the most comprehensive approach to instruction? That would be the *Common Core Curriculum Maps* project produced by the organization Common Core and published by Jossey Bass. Common Core is a nonprofit group established in 2007 to "advocate for a content-rich liberal arts education in America's K–12 schools" (Common Core 2012, 405). Its president and executive director is Lynne Munson, a former deputy chair of the National Endowment for the Humanities and research fellow at the conservative American Enterprise Institute think tank. The lessons included in the curriculum maps were written by several public school teachers, many of whom are associated with organizations such as Achieve, the Education Trust, the Fordham Foundation, Teach for America, and E. D. Hirsch's Core Knowledge Foundation.

In its current iteration, these "maps" consist of a series of approximately six interdisciplinary, language arts–based units at each K–12 grade level. Each unit consists of an essential question, a list of standards and objectives addressed, thirty to forty suggested texts, ten to twenty sample activities/assessments, a list of key terminology, a sample lesson plan, and outlines for two to ten follow-up lessons. In summer 2010, Common

Core released these units with the claim that "any teacher who chooses to follow these maps would not have to worry about whether they were addressing all of the standards that apply to their grade" (Hahn 2010). The units were initially available for free on the group's website and were originally touted as an answer to rising district curriculum costs. But Common Core is ambitious. The group intends to develop maps in the areas of mathematics and social studies and provide professional development to guide groups of teachers as they develop additional lessons; the end goal is to realize their vision for a "complete curriculum" which would include more fully crafted lesson plans, detailed suggestions for differentiation, a scope and sequence, student work samples, scoring rubrics, pacing guides, vocabulary lists, assessment blueprints, and detailed recommendations for grammar instruction (Common Core 2012). In service of this vision, they now charge a twenty-five dollar membership fee to access resources via the online site and also sell hard-copy versions of the K–5, 6–8, and 9–12 maps for about thirty dollars each.

Because most of my teaching experience has been in the upper elementary grades, I turned to Common Core's Fourth Grade Unit 1 as my exemplar. The unit is called "Tales of the Heart" and it "invites students to explore the mixture of emotions that accompany the transition to fourth grade, as well as to learn from informational text about the body" (Common Core 2012, 269). There are nineteen standards addressed and eighteen activities/assessments recommended (including six genres of writing). Eight pages into the unit, I discover the sample lesson plan with follow-up lesson outlines, and who do I find there but Jack and Miss Stretchberry. What goes on in these lessons? What do teachers teach and what, for better or worse, are children (and their teachers) likely to learn?

## CHILDREN LEARN . . .

I receive a folder containing eight poems; the teacher tells us to "study" them. I learn that poems are commodities; more equals more, and maybe all are interchangeable. I learn that poems are to be looked at.

One of my classmates reads the first poem aloud. I learn each poem comes in one voice and, if I want that voice to be mine, I better raise my hand up quick.

I write what I think about the poem and I discuss it. I learn that whenever I study a poem, I need to know what it means, have an opinion about it lickety-split, and be willing to compare my knowledge and opinions with others (even if they feel too personal to share).

I continue to read Jack's letters and try to figure out what Miss Stretchberry must have said in response. *I learn that there is more to what goes on in a story than what is printed on the page.*

I trace the subplot. *I learn that there can be stories within stories.*

I discern Jack's views on poetry and compare them to my own. I learn that nine-year-olds should have an opinion about literary genres considered in the abstract.

I reflect on Jack's decision to identify himself as the author of his poems. *I learn that I can choose my identity as a poet.*

I write a brief poem, emulating "The Red Wheelbarrow." I learn that when I consume a poem, I must then produce something similar; I learn that I am not capable of making my own choices about poetic form.

I classify examples of rhyme schemes, alliteration, similes, and metaphors in the poems we have studied. I learn that poems are amalgamations of literary devices.

If I am a struggling reader, I listen to the poems on tape and draw a picture to go with them. If I am an advanced reader, I conduct research on a poet of my choice and share it with my friends via a multimedia presentation. I learn that children for whom school comes easily get rewarded with sophisticated projects over which they have considerable control; children for whom school is a challenge get simple assignments and are expected to do as they are told.

Students in a language arts classroom organized around units from the *Common Core Curriculum Maps* will learn some valuable things; those in italics above seem particularly so. But they will also take away some messages about the enjoyment and crafting of poetry that will not serve them. And of the experiences they have and the understandings they gain, how much of it is fundamentally different from what has gone on in classrooms across the country prior to the CCSS?

## . . . AND TEACHERS LEARN . . .

Teachers who consider employing these tools—ranging from less to more market-driven—will also learn from them. From Calkins and her colleagues they learn that, whatever one's ambivalence about the CCSS, the best approach is to set aside those concerns and get with the program, albeit by developing one's own lessons; Owocki skips the concerns part entirely. From LearnZillion and Share My Lesson, teachers learn that the most important thing about teaching is deciding what one will do on Monday and that the content and quality of these lessons, as well as the soundness of long-term planning, is largely irrelevant. From Common Core they learn that, once given a model lesson and a list of key components, they are capable only of mimicking this lesson for other standards and content areas. From McGraw-Hill they learn two things: that flash is more important than substance, and that it is most effective and efficient to turn responsibility for instructional decision making over to a major player in the educational marketplace and just do what they are told. And what they learn overall is that, as new as the CCSS appear to be, education is a business-as-usual proposition. We can get by teaching in the ways we have always taught. The content may be slightly different but the instructional environment changes not a whit.

I am not an ardent CCSS foe, nor am I an advocate. The questions I ask myself when I think about the standards and examine the instructional materials developed in response to them—particularly the more prescriptive, market-driven ones—are quite simple: Is it likely that children will read and write more effectively—and engage in the acts of reading and writing more happily—than before these materials graced their teachers' desks? Will their lives be richer? Will they be more able participants in a democracy? The *answers* to these questions are, of course, less simple, because the quality of published materials varies quite dramatically. But as I analyze the lessons based on *Love That Dog* as developed for the *Common Core Curriculum Maps* project, my answer is, essentially, no. They will not see poetry as a largely oral genre to be read over and over in a variety of voices as part of a classroom community. They will not come to believe that both the content and form of poetry can be fully within their control. They will likely not seek out other poems to make their own. And they will not write in ways that allow them to make sense of their world.

# CHAPTER 9

## *Teachers as the Standard(s) Bearers*

>> CURT DUDLEY-MARLING

*Who will we blame when the Common Core leaves some students behind?*

I have a good friend who is an enthusiastic supporter of the Common Core State Standards (CCSS). My friend is a smart, productive scholar whose judgment I tend to trust. She is convinced that the emphasis on claims and evidence throughout the CCSS provide an opportunity for creating challenging curriculum that will encourage higher levels of student engagement and learning. When I've countered with my more pessimistic view that, whatever richness the standards possess, they will likely be corrupted by the tests that will be used to measure the effect of CCSS-based curriculum, she shares her faith that the new generation of tests being developed to align with the CCSS will be different. Perhaps. I believe, however, that our collective experience over the last twenty years or so indicates that high standards and testing linked to those standards have never done much to improve the quality of schooling. Nor have high standards ever done much to improve the professional lives of teachers. Even if the CCSS and the new generation of tests that will be used to assess the standards are an improvement over whatever it is they replace, the current context of education policy making that seeks to transform schools through market-based reforms that emphasize competition, choice, and hyperaccountability remains in place.

In this brief essay, I consider our previous experience with standards and testing as well as the current context of education reform to predict the effect that I think the CCSS will have on teachers and students. Many people no doubt share my friend's hopes for the CCSS but, given the history of standards and testing in the United States, I find it difficult to be optimistic.

## TEACHERS AS THE STANDARD(S) BEARERS

> The standards clearly communicate what is expected of students at each grade level. This will allow our teachers to be better equipped to know exactly what they need to help students learn and establish individualized benchmarks for them. (National Governors Association Center for Best Practices, Council of Chief State School Officers, 2010)

I do not reject standards. Standards matter. Teachers must know what they're aiming for if they're going to provide students with appropriate instruction. This is especially important in poor, low-achieving schools that have been plagued by low expectations. Students also need to know what's expected of them. I can also see why my friend is hopeful about the CCSS for English language arts given the emphasis on reading comprehension; the close reading of complex, challenging texts; expanding the range of genres students read and write; and the demand for interdisciplinary connections. I see a ray of hope in the observation that the CCSS may move schools away from the emphasis on low-level skills inspired by NCLB and the report of the National Reading Panel toward a more holistic, text-based approach to reading instruction (Gewertz 2012; Sparks 2012).

Still, I'm uneasy with these standards, particularly the form the CCSS have taken. I worry about negative effects the CCSS may have on teachers. Consider the standard for literacy in third grade:

> By the end of the year, read and comprehend literature, including stories, dramas, and poetry, at the high end of the grades 2–3 text complexity band independently and proficiently. (National Governors Association Center for Best Practices, Council of Chief State School Officers, 2010)

There are two different ways of thinking about standards. We can have broad-brush standards that give teachers and students a sense of what they are aspiring toward. It's a goal but it is not an expectation that all students will necessarily achieve. For instance, we want to provide every student with challenging curricula that gives them the opportunity to achieve at a level that gives them access to higher education even if we don't actually expect all children to go to college. Ambitious goals and challenging, high-expectation curricula have been found to dramatically affect the achievement of students in low-achieving, high-poverty schools (Dudley-Marling and Michaels 2012). From this perspective, high standards are welcome.

Alternatively, standards can be viewed as minimum expectations that every student should be able to achieve. We expect, for example, that every student will achieve at least a basic level of competence in literacy, although the meaning of "basic" has proved to be nettlesome. The problem arises when *high standards* are conflated with minimum expectations, and this is what worries me about the CCSS. Consider, for instance, the standard I referenced above that "by the end of the year" children in third grade will independently read text at "the high end of the grades 2–3 text complexity band." Since claims about grade levels typically reference normative assumptions (i.e., a third-grade reading level is generally understood as the average level of reading achievement for third graders), is it reasonable or even possible to expect all third-grade students will achieve at the "upper band" for third graders? Isn't this tantamount to saying that we'd like all third graders to be above average? Or, if all third graders can reasonably be expected to achieve in the "upper band," is this really a high standard? If the standard describes something that everyone can do it sounds to me like a minimum expectation, not a high standard. And if everyone is able to somehow achieve at the "upper band" for second and third graders it seems that this would shift what counts as the "upper band" ever higher. Here we have a conundrum.

It seems pretty clear from the language of the CCSS, which indicates what students are expected to know "by the end of the year," that the standards will be interpreted as minimum expectations for all students. This sense is further reinforced by the specificity of the standards. One of the standards for fourth graders, for example, is that they "use combined knowledge of all letter-sound correspondences, syllabication patterns, and morphology (e.g., roots and affixes) to read accurately unfamiliar multisyllabic words in context and out of context." This doesn't sound like a broad-brush standard that students and teachers should aspire to. The specificity of this standard—and other standards in the Common Core—guarantees that students will be tested to see if they have mastered this knowledge and that students and teachers will be held accountable for whether this level of mastery has been achieved.

Again, I'm not resisting the idea of high standards for all students, only the implicit claim in the CCSS that all children will achieve at the highest levels or that high standards are sufficient for ameliorating the achievement gap. I am firmly committed to the idea that all students are entitled to the same rich, engaging curricula that are found in high-achieving, typically affluent schools. But the evidence from my home state of Massachusetts, which is acknowledged to have very high standards, is not encouraging. Despite the presence of high standards in the form of state-mandated curricular frameworks and challenging statewide assessments, students in high-poverty schools in Massachusetts still experience curricula focused on low-level skills. More to the point, high standards in Massachusetts have not eliminated the achievement gap between high-poverty schools overpopulated by students of color and more affluent, high-achieving schools overpopulated by white students.

So what will happen when a significant proportion of third graders don't "read and comprehend literature . . . at the high end of the grades 2–3 text complexity band independently and proficiently" or when a fifth grader can't "determine a theme of a story, drama, or poem from details in the text, including how characters in a story or drama respond to challenges or how the speaker in a poem reflects upon a topic?" How will policy makers, politicians, and the public respond when the new generation of tests aligned with the CCSS determine that many students failed to achieve the high standards of the Common Core? How will these same groups react when high standards fail to overcome the material effects of poverty and close the achievement gap? Will policy makers and politicians conclude that the standards were too challenging or that the standards were just general goals? Will they cite the intractable effects of poverty, insufficient funding, or inadequate professional development? Of course, we know the answer to these questions. In the thirty years since the publication of *A Nation at Risk* (National Commission on Excellence in Education 1983) the blame for the perceived failures of American schools has fallen on teachers who have "low expectations." At best, the CCSS will be another burden teachers must endure. Teachers will be the bearers of the standards in the most literal sense. At worst, the standards will be a cudgel with which to continue the assault on teachers and the teaching profession. I wish I could share my friend's optimism that the CCSS will have a liberating effect on teachers and students, but history tells me otherwise.

## NEW GENERATION OF TESTS

Few would disagree that the current generation of high-stakes tests has led to low-level, teach-to-the-test curricula that has undermined the quality of schooling for many students, especially students in underfunded, low-achieving schools overpopulated by students of color (Gordon Commission on the Future of Education 2012; Nicols and Berliner 2007). Moreover, the summative nature of current state- and district-mandated high-stakes tests fails to provide much in the way of useful data. Here in Massachusetts, for example, the state tests (the Massachusetts Comprehensive Assessment System [MCAS]) are administered each spring in math and English language arts in grades 3–8 and grade 10. When the results of MCAS are released in the fall, principals and teachers pore over the test data looking for useful data to inform instruction. There are, however, some serious flaws in this process. First, the data come too late to be useful to individual teachers and students. When a third-grade teacher, for example, reviews the data for her class, her students have already moved on to fourth grade. And the purpose of summative tests like the MCAS, which provide snapshots of student learning at various stages, is in conflict with the purpose of formative evaluations which focus on gathering data needed to improve the quality of instruction for individual students. One test cannot fulfill the purposes of summative and formative evaluation.

According to the Massachusetts Department of Elementary and Secondary Education website the purpose of the MCAS is "to inform/improve curriculum and instruction." But how? Clearly the nature of these tests is inadequate to inform day-to-day instruction. A recent article in *Education Week* quotes an expert on educational testing who argues that the problem is that educational policy makers confuse summative and formative evaluation because of "misbeliefs" leading to the focus on low-level skills and teach-to-the-test curriculum (Sparks 2012, 8). I believe, however, that this situation has less to do with policy makers' "misbeliefs" than testing experts' misapprehensions about the intentions of policy makers. The intentions of policy makers have to be understood in the context of the discourse of education reform that identifies teachers as the problem. The implication of routine achievement testing in this context is that teachers cannot be trusted to do their own assessments. Ultimately, the problem isn't data but teachers who presumably can be motivated only by the threat of sanctions to do what's best for their students. For this reason, policy makers want high-stakes tests with consequences. Underlying the demand that states receiving RTTT funds must implement teacher evaluation schemes which include the use of student test scores is the belief that "teachers need to be held accountable through high-stakes tests to motivate them to teach better and to push the lazy ones to work harder" (Nichols and Berliner 2007, 94). The real purpose of these tests is the surveillance and control of teachers who cannot be trusted to act in the best interests of their students.

It has been claimed that the new generation of tests will be based on a "new vision for an aligned system of standards, assessment, and curriculum" (Gordon Commission on the Future of Assessment in Education 2012). The new tests will be administered online and, therefore, will be more efficient—and results will be available to teachers sooner. They will also provide more precise, reliable assessment data (Davis 2012). But in the presence of the demand for tests with high stakes this new generation of tests will corrupt the teaching and learning process in the same way current tests do. The new tests will, however, be more efficient at surveilling and controlling the work of teachers.

Certainly, ongoing assessment is a critical part of effective instruction. Good teachers provide instruction that responds to the needs of their students, which is possible only if they are routinely assessing their students' progress. However, given the recent history of high-stakes testing in the

United States and the current context of hyperaccountability that dominates the education landscape, it's easy to predict that, in the likely scenario that the CCSS fail to lift achievement in high-poverty schools, the new tests will function mainly as evidence of the failure of teachers.

The main reason for my pessimism about how the CCSS and the tests aligned with those standards will be used is that the actual meaning of the standards and tests will be a function of the context in which they are implemented—and new standards and new tests do nothing to reverse the rise of market-based schooling in this country. Indeed, *common* standards and *common* tests unwittingly (or maybe wittingly) support the spread of market-based school reforms.

## THE COMMON CORE AND THE FREE MARKET

Writing over fifty years ago, Milton Friedman (1955) argued that the most effective means for reforming American education is to expose schools to the competitive forces of the free market—providing a powerful incentive for schools to be efficient and effective in contrast to traditional public schools that, as monopolies, have no such incentives. Apple (1996) observed that a national curriculum and testing program are essential steps toward implementing Friedman's vision of market-based schooling. *Common* assessments of *common* curricula provide the objective data required to make teachers accountable and to enable parents (read: consumers) to make informed choices about the best schools for their children. In this way, the market works its magic as parents flock to the most effective schools—and less effective schools, those that fail to attract students, close. Rigid accountability procedures, facilitated by standard forms of assessment based on comparable curricular practices, presumably ensure that the most effective schools are staffed by the best teachers whose students achieve the highest test scores (Hursh 2007).

The move toward more standardized practices achieves another market imperative: reducing costs and, in the case of for-profit charter schools, increasing profits (Zollers and Ramanathan 1998). In a free-market model of schooling, teachers are reduced to commodities whose value is derived from their students' test scores. This does not, however, necessarily lead to higher pay and status for teachers. The same market forces that reduce teachers to commodities may also rob them of their status as knowledgeable professionals. In a market economy there is every incentive to reduce employment costs and one way to accomplish that is by adopting scripted curricula for which well-educated, well-paid teachers are not required. It is no surprise that Edison Schools, perhaps the largest private operator of charter schools in the United States, uses scripted reading programs—*Open Court* and *Success for All*—in all of its schools (Wyckoff and Doerman 2007).

To return to the friend who I cited at the beginning of this essay—she recently forwarded to me a petition calling for an end to high-stakes testing in Massachusetts. This strongly suggests that she recognizes that for the CCSS to fulfill its promise, the standards cannot be yoked to high-stakes testing. And this is precisely my point. In the context of free-market schooling with the emphasis on "accountability, high-stakes testing, data-driven decision making, choice, charter schools, privatization, deregulation, merit pay, and competition among schools" (Ravitch 2010, 21), teachers are transformed into low-level technicians who follow the curriculum and whose value is derived from student test scores. In the final analysis, the CCSS facilitate the move toward a national curriculum and national testing that may further accelerate the marketization of American schools. This is not good news for teachers.

# AFTERWORD

## *You Are Here—Where Would You Like to Be?*

As this book goes to press, state CCS testing has started in Kentucky and New York. The results have been predictable—proficiency rates dropped between 50 and 30 percentage points. Advocates conclude that this evidence demonstrates the need for the CCS Standards and the aligned system, but others question the practice of employing a test of content not yet added to the curriculum. Think about that for a minute.

The contributors to this text invite you to ask such questions about the Common Core Standards in relationship to the children, adolescents, and teachers who will live among CCS. How does it feel to be tested on something for which you haven't had the opportunity to learn? What does the mismatch mean to teachers whose evaluations will be based on the outcome? When do you break the news to parents? Why do such a thing? Who could benefit and who could be harmed?

Such big questions are neither rhetorical nor negative. They simply treat the CCS Standards as a text and take the Standards for reading seriously. Anchor standard #8 states:

> delineate and evaluate the argument and specific claims in a text, including the validity of the reasoning as well as the relevance and sufficiency of the evidence.

Go ahead. Show them that you can carry this Standard!

# REFERENCES

Achieve. 2004. "Ready or Not: Creating a High School Diploma That Counts." Accessed October 10, 2012. www.isbe.net/common_core/pdf/ADP_benchmarks.pdf.

———. 2008. "Out of Many, One: Toward Rigorous Common Core Standards from the Ground Up." Accessed October 10, 2012. www.achieve.org/outofmanyone.

Achieve the Core. (n.d.) Common Core Professional Development. (Retrieved from www.achievethecore.org/steal-these-tools/professional-development-modules.)

Achieve and U.S. Education Delivery Institute. 2012. Implementing Common Core State Standards and Assessments: A Workbook for State and District Leaders. (Retrieved at http://www.achieve.org/files/Common_Core_Workbook.pdf.

Achivethecore.org. 2012. "Student Achievement Partners: Close Reading Exemplars." Accessed December 2, 2012. www.achievethecore.org/steal-these-tools/close-reading -exemplars.

Adams, M. J., 2009. The challenge of advanced texts: The interdependence of reading and learning. In E. H. Hiebert (Ed.), *Reading more, reading better: Are American students reading enough of the right stuff?* (pp. 163–189). New York, NY: Guilford.

Albers, P. 2004. "Literacy in Art: A Question of Responsibility." *Democracy and Education* 15 (3–4): 32–41.

———. 2007. "Visual Discourse Analysis: An Introduction to the Analysis of School Generated Visual Texts." In *56th Yearbook of the National Reading Conference*, edited by D. W. Rowe, R. T. Jimenez, D. L. Compton, D. K. Dickinson, Y. Kim, K. M. Leander, and V. J. Risko, 81–95. Oak Creek, WI: National Reading Conference.

———. 2011. "Double Exposure: A Critical Study of Preservice Teachers' Multimodal Public Service Announcements." *Multimodal Communication* 1 (1): 47–64.

Apple, M. W. 1996. *Cultural Politics and Education.* Buckingham, UK: Open University Press.

Baker, B., and R. Ferris. 2011. *Adding Up the Spending: Fiscal Disparity and Philanthropy Among New York City Charter Schools*, January. National Education Policy Center. Accessed October 21, 2012. http://nepc.colorado.edu/files/NEPC -NYCharter-Baker-Ferris.pdf.

Beach, R. 2011. "Analyzing How Formalist, Cognitive Processing, and Literacy Practices Learning Paradigms Are Shaping the Implementation of the Common Core Standards." Paper presented at the annual meeting of the Literacy Research Association, Jacksonville, FL, December 2.

Beach, R., A. H. Thein, and A. Webb. 2012. *Teaching to Exceed the English Language Arts Common Core Standards: A Literacy Practices Approach for 6–12 Classrooms.* New York: Routledge.

Beaufort, A. 2007. *College Writing and Beyond: A New Framework for University Writing Instruction.* Logan, UT: Utah State University Press.

Berliner, D. 2009. *Poverty and Potential: Out of School Factors and School Success.* National Education Policy Center. Accessed October 2, 2012. http://nepc.colorado .edu/publication/poverty-and-potential.

Berliner, D. C., and B. J. Biddle. 1995. *The Manufactured Crisis: Myths, Fraud, and the Attack on America's Public Schools.* Reading, MA: Addison-Wesley Publishing.

Berry, B., J. Eckert, and S. Bauries. 2012. *Creating Teacher Incentives for School Excellence and Equity*, January. National Education Policy Center. Accessed October 21, 2012. http://nepc.colorado.edu/publication/creating-teacher-incentives.

Bomer, R., J. Dworin, L. May, and P. Semingson. 2008. "Miseducating Teachers About the Poor: A Critical Analysis of Ruby Payne's Claims About Poverty." *Teachers College Record* 110: 2497–2531.

Borman, G. D., M. N. Dowling, and C. Schneck. 2008. "A Multi-site Cluster Randomized Field Trial of *Open Court Reading.*" *Educational Evaluation and Policy Analysis* 30 (4): 389–407.

Bowles, S., and H. Gintis. 1976. *Schooling in Capitalist America: Educational Reform and the Contradictions of Economic Life.* New York: Basic.

Bracey, G. 2009. *The Bracey Report on the Condition of Public Education.* National Education Policy Center. Accessed October 2, 2012. http://nepc.colorado.edu/files /BRACEY-2009.pdf.

Brown, C. 2009. "Pivoting a Pre-kindergarten Program off the Child or the Standard? A Case Study of Integrating the Practices of Early Childhood Education into Elementary School." *Elementary School Journal* 110: 202–227.

———. 2010. "Balancing the Readiness Equation in Early Childhood Education Reform." *Journal of Early Childhood Research* 8: 133–60.

Calkins, L., M. Ehrenworth, and C. Lehman. 2012. *Pathways to the Common Core: Accelerating Achievement.* Portsmouth, NH: Heinemann.

Callahan, R. 1962. *Education and the Cult of Efficiency.* Chicago: University of Chicago.

Chang, H. J. 2010. *23 Things They Don't Tell You About Capitalism.* New York: Bloomsbury.

Chase, M. 2012. "Revision Process and Practice: A Kindergarten Experience." *Language Arts* 89 (3): 166–78.

Clark, B. 1980. *Whose Life Is It Anyway?* Woodstock, IL: Dramatic Pub. Co.

Cochran-Smith, M., and S. Lytle. 2009. *Inquiry as Stance.* New York: Teachers College.

Coleman, D. 2011a. "Bringing Common Core to Life." Accessed October 17, 2012. http://vimeo.com/25242442.

Coleman, D. 2011b. "Presentation to the New York State Department of Education." Accessed October 17, 2012. http://www.schoolsmatter.info/2012/04/david -colemans-global-revenge-and.html.

Coleman, D., and S. Pimentel. 2011. "Publishers' Criteria for the Common Core State Standards in English Language Arts and Literacy, Grades 3–12." Accessed July 2, 2012. http://usny.nysed.gov/rttt/docs/publisherscriteria-literacy-gradesk-2.pdf

———. 2012a. "Revised Publishers' Criteria for the Common Core State Standards in English Language Arts and Literacy, Grades 3–12." Accessed July 2, 2012. www.corestandards.org/assets/Publishers_Criteria_for_3-12.pdf.

———. 2012b. "Revised Publishers' Criteria for the Common Core State Standards in English Language Arts and Literacy, Grades K–2." Accessed November 5, 2012. www.corestandards.org/assets/Publishers_Criteria_for_K-2.pdf.

Common Core. 2012. *Common Core Curriculum Maps, K–5: English Language Arts.* San Francisco, CA: Jossey-Bass.

Common Core Standards. 2010. "Common Core Standards for English Language Arts." Accessed November 30, 2012. www.corestandards.org/.

Common Core State Standards in the English Language Arts and Literacy: List of Text Exemplars—Appendix B. 2012. Accessed November 5, 2012. www.corestandards .org/assets/Appendix_B.pdf.

Common Core State Standards Initiative. n.d. English Language Arts Standards >> Introduction >> Key Design Considerations. Accessed November 12, 2012. www .corestandards.org/ELA-Literacy/introduction/key-design-consideration.

Common Core State Standards Initiative. 2010. "Common Core State Standards for English Language Arts and Literacy in History/Social Studies, Science, and Technical Subjects." Accessed February 1, 2011. http://corestandards.org/assets/CCSSI _ELA%20 Standards.pdf.

Common Core State Standards Validation Committee. 2010. "Reaching Higher: Common Core State Standards Initiative." Accessed October 11, 2012. www.corestandards.org/assets/CommonCoreReport_6.10.pdf.

Common Core State Standards Initiative. (n.d.). *Myths vs. Facts.* (Retrieved from http://www.corestandards.org/about-the-standards/myths-vs-facts.)

Cook, C. November, 2012. "The Progressive Interview with Robert Reich." *The Progressive,* 76, 11, 36.

Creech, S. 2001. *Love That Dog.* New York: Harper Collins.

Cuban, L. 2010. "Common Core Standards: Hardly an Evidence Based Policy." Accessed January 5, 2013. http://larrycuban.wordpress.com/2010/07/25/common-core -standards-hardly-an-evidence-based-policy/.

Curtis, M., and A. Herrington. 2003. "Writing Development in the College Years: By Whose Definition?" *College Composition and Communication*, 55 (1): 69–90.

Davis, M. R. 2012. "Shifting to Adaptive Testing." *Education Week: Digital Directions* 6 (1): 12–16.

Dewey, J. 1899. *School in Society*. Chicago: University of Chicago.

Douglass, F. 1845. *Narrative of the Life of Frederick Douglass, an American Slave*. Boston, MA: Anti-Slavery Office, No. 25, Cornhill. Accessed December 2, 2012. www.ibiblio.org/ebooks/Douglass/Narrative/Douglass_Narrative.pdf.

Drum, Kevin. 2012. "The Kids Are All Right: Students Score Better Today Than You Did." *Mother Jones*, September/October. Accessed October 2, 2012. www.motherjones.com/politics/2012/08/kids-school-test-scores-charts-kevin-drum.

Dudley-Marling, C., and S. Michaels, eds. 2012. *High-Expectation Curricula: Help All Students Succeed with Powerful Learning*. New York: Teachers College Press.

Eisner, E. 2002. "What Can Education Learn from the Arts About the Practice of Education?" *Journal of Curriculum and Supervision* 18 (1): 4–16.

Fish, S. 1980. *Is There a Text in This Class?* Cambridge, MA: Harvard University Press.

Fishman, J., A. Lunsford, B. McGregor, and M. Otuteye. 2005. "Performing Writing, Performing Literacy." *College Composition and Communication*, 57: 224–52.

Frady, M. 2005. *Martin Luther King, Jr.: A Life*. New York: Penguin.

Friedman, M. 1955. "The Role of Government in Education." In *Economics and the Public Interest*, edited by R. A. Solo. New Brunswick, NJ: Rutgers University Press. Accessed May 14, 2013. https://webspace.utexas.edu/hcleaver/www/FriedmanRoleOfGovtEducation1955.htm.

Friedman, T. 2012. "So Much Fun; So Irrelevant." Editorial. *The New York Times*, January 3, A13.

Gates, B. 2009. Address to the National Conference of State Legislatures. Accessed October 2, 2012. www.youtube.com/watch?v=xtTK_6VKpf4&feature=relmfu.

GE Foundation. 2012. "Developing Futures in Education Initiative." Accessed October 7, 2012. www.ge.com/foundation/developing_futures_in_education/index.jsp.

Gee, J. 1985. "The Narrativization of Experience in Oral Style." *Journal of Education*, 167, 9–35.

Gee, J. 1999. *An Introduction to Discourse Analysis: Theory and Method*. London, UK: Routledge.

Gee, J. 2004. *Situated Language and Learning: A Critique of Traditional Schooling*. New York: Routledge.

Gewertz, C. 2012a. "Incoming College Board Head Wants SAT to Reflect Common Core." *Education Week*, May 16. Accessed December 2. www.edweek.org/ew/articles/2012/05/16/32collegeboard.h31.html.

Gewertz, C. 2012b. "Teachers Embedding Standards in Basal-Reader Questions." *Education Week*, April 26. Accessed December 2, 2012. www.edweek.org/ew /articles/2012/04/26/30basal.h31.html.

Gewertz, C. 2012c. "Common Standards Drive New Reading Approaches." *Education Week*. Accessed January 11, 2013. www.edweek.org/go/common-reading.

Gillen, J., and G. Merchant. 2013. "Contact Calls: Twitter as a Dialogic Social and Linguistic Practice." *Language Sciences* 35: 3547–58.

Goldin, C., and L. Katz. 2008. *The Race Between Education and Technology.* New York: Belnap.

Goldstein, L. 2007. "Embracing Pedagogical Multiplicity: Examining Two Teachers' Instructional Responses to the Changing Expectations for Kindergarten in U.S. Public Schools." *Journal of Research in Childhood Education* 21: 388–400.

Gonzalez, N., L. C. Moll, and C. Amanti. 2005. *Funds of Knowledge: Theorizing Practices in Households, Communities, and Classrooms.* New York: Teachers College Press.

Gordon Commission on the Future of Assessment in Education. 2012. "Shifting Paradigms: Beyond the Abstract." Accessed November 14, 2012. www .gordoncommission.org.

Grant, A., F. Gino, and A. Hofman. 2010. "The Hidden Advantages of Quiet Bosses." *Harvard Business Review: The Magazine*, December. Accessed December 2, 2012. http://hbr.org/2010/12/the-hidden-advantages-of-quiet-bosses/ar/1.

Greene, M. 1978. *Landscapes of Learning.* New York: Teachers College Press.

———. 1995. *Releasing the Imagination.* San Francisco, CA: Jossey-Bass.

Hahn, J. S. 2010. "Curriculum Maps Based on Common Core Standards Released for Public Feedback." Accessed November 7, 2012. www.susanohanian.org/core .php?id=45.

Halliday, M.A. K. 1978. *Language as Social Semiotic: The Social Interpretation of Language and Meaning.* London: Edward Arnold.

Hammond, L. D. 2010. *The Flat World and Education.* New York: Teachers College.

Hatch, J. A. 2002. "Accountability Shovedown: Resisting the Standards Movement in Education." *Phi Delta Kappan* 83: 457–63.

Heath, S. B. 1983. *Ways With Words: Language, Life, and Work in Communities and Classrooms.* New York: Cambridge University Press.

Heilig, J., and S. Jez. 2010. *Teach for America: A Review of the Evidence*, June. National Education Policy Center. Accessed October 21, 2012. http://nepc.colorado.edu /publication/teach-for-america.

Hess, R. 2010. *Same Old Thing Over and Over: How School Reformers Get Stuck in Yesterday's Ideas.* Cambridge, MA: Harvard University.

———. 2012. "Straight up Conversation: Common Core Architect and New College Board President David Coleman." *Education Week.* Accessed October 10, 2012. http://blogs.edweek.org/edweek/rick_hess_straight_up/2012/06/straight_up_conversation_common_core_architect_and_new_college_board_president_david_coleman.html.

Hill, G. 2009. "Media Images: Do They Influence College Students' Body Image?" *Journal of Family and Consumer Sciences* 101 (2): 28–32.

Hobbs, R., and R. Frost. 2003. "Measuring the Acquisition of Media-Literacy Skills." *Reading Research Quarterly* 38 (3): 330–54.

Hodge, R., and G. Kress. 1996. *Social Semiotics.* Ithaca, NY: Cornell University Press.

Hursh, D. 2007. "Exacerbating Inequality: The Failed Promise of the No Child Left Behind Act." *Race, Ethnicity and Education* 10 (3): 295–308.

Isadora, Rachel. 2008. *The Fisherman and His Wife.* New York: Putnam's.

Janks, H. and V. Vasquez, 2011. Critical literacy revisited: Writing as critique. *English Teaching: Practice and Critique, 10*(1), 1–6.

Keats, E. J. 1962. *The Snowy Day.* New York: Puffin Books.

Kilgour-Dowdy, J. 2012. *Artful Stories: The Teacher, the Student, and the Muse.* New York: Peter Lang.

King, C. 2012. "Readers Rapidly Gravitate to E-books." *The Washington Post,* Accessed December 28, 2012. http://articles.washingtonpost.com/2012-12-27/business/36015490_1_major-book-publishers-digital-books-e-book-sales.

Klein, A. 2010. "State Policymakers Talk Standards, Race to the Top, ESEA, Politics K–12." *Education Week.* Accessed October 10, 2012. http://blogs.edweek.org/edweek/campaign-k-12/2010/08/school_chiefs_and_govs_talk_es.html.

Klein, J., and C. Rice. 2012. *U. S. Education Reform and National Security.* Washington, DC: Council on Foreign Relations.

Krashen, S., S. Lee, and J. McQuillan. 2010. "An Analysis of PIRLS 2006 Data: Can the School Library Reduce the Effects of Poverty on Reading Achievement." *California School Library Association Journal* 34: 26–28. Accessed October 2, 2012. www.ala.org/aasl/sites/ala.org.aasl/files/content/aaslissues/advocacy/Krashen_Lee_McQuillan_PIRLS.pdf.

Kress, G., and T. van Leeuwen. 2006. *Reading Images: The Grammar of Visual Design* (2nd ed.). New York: Routledge.

Lakoff, G. 2004. *Don't Think of an Elephant: Know Your Values and Frame the Debate.* White River, VT: Chelsea Green Publishing.

Lakoff, G., and M. Johnson. 2003. *Metaphors We Live By.* Chicago, IL: University of Chicago Press.

Lankshear, C., and M. Knobel. 2006. *New Literacies: Everyday Practices and Classroom Learning.* Maidenhead, England: Open University Press.

Larson, L. C. 2013. "It's Time to Turn the Digital Page: Preservice Teachers Explore E-book Reading." *Journal of Adolescent and Adult Literacy* 56 (4): 280–90.

Leigh, S. R. 2012. "Writers Draw Visual Hooks." *Language Arts* 89 (6): 396–404.

Leu, D. L., Jr., C. K. Kinzer, J. L. Coiro, and D. W. Cammack. 2004. "Toward a Theory of New Literacies Emerging from the Internet and Other Information and Communication Technologies." In *Theoretical Models and Processes of Reading* (5th ed.), edited by N. J. Unrau and R. B. Rudell, 1570–1613. Newark, DE: International Reading Association.

Lewin, T. 2010. "Many States Adopt National Standards for Their Schools." The *New York Times*, July 21, A1.

Loveless, T. 2012. *How Well Are American Students Learning?* The Brown Center Report on American Education, Washington, DC: Brookings Institute.

Mallozzi, C. A. 2011. "Reading Women Teachers: A Theoretical Assertion for Bodies as Texts." *English Teaching: Practice and Critique* 10 (3): 129–41.

McGraw-Hill Education. 2013. "About Us." Accessed November 14, 2012. www.mheducation.com/aboutus/index.shtml.

McLaughlin, M., and B. J. Overturf. 2012. *The Common Core: Teaching K–5 Students to Meet the Reading Standards.* Newark, DE: International Reading Association.

Merriam-Webster Online Dictionary. Accessed January 7, 2013. www.merriam webster .com/dictionary/standard.

Michaels, S. 1981. "'Sharing Time': Children's Narrative Styles and Differential Access to Literacy." *Language in Society* 10 (3): 423–42.

Miron, G., J. Urschel, W. Mathis, and E. Tornquist. 2010, *Schools Without Diversity: Education Management Organizations, Charter Schools and Demographic Stratification.* February. National Educational Policy Center. Accessed October 21, 2012. http://nepc.colorado.edu/publication/schools-without-diversity.

Moll, L., C. Amanti, D. Neff, and N. Gonzalez. 1992. "Funds of Knowledge for Teaching: Using a Quantitative Approach to Connect Homes and Classrooms." 31 (2): 131–41.

Murphy, S. 2012. "Reclaiming Pleasure in the Teaching of Reading." *Language Arts* 89 (5): 318–28.

Nathan Love. 2012. "Nathan Love Website." Accessed January 11, 2013. http:// m.nathanlove.com/.

National Commission on Excellence in Education. 1983. *A Nation at Risk: The Imperative for Educational Reform.* Washington, DC: United States Department of Education. Accessed October 17, 2012. http://datacenter.spps.org/uploads /SOTW_A_Nation_at_Risk_1983.pdf.

National Council of Education Standards and Testing. 1992. *Raising Standards for American Education.* Washington, DC: U.S. Government Printing Office.

National Council of Teachers of English. 2006. "Principles of Professional Development." Accessed January 12, 2013. www.ncte.org/positions/statements/profdevelopment.

National Governors Association Center for Best Practices, Council of Chief State School Officers. 2010. *Common Core State Standards (English Language Arts)*. Washington, DC: Council of Chief State School Officers. Accessed December 2, 2012. www.corestandards.org/assets/CCSSI_ELA%20Standards.pdf.

National Governors Association Center for Best Practices, Council of Chief State School Officers. 2010. *Common Core State Standards for English Language Arts & Literacy in History/Social Studies, Science, and Technical Subjects Appendix A: Research Supporting Key Elements of the Standards*. National Governors Association Center for Best Practices, Council of Chief State School Officers, Washington, D.C.

National Institute of Child Health and Human Development. 2000. *Teaching Children to Read: An Evidence-Based Assessment of the Scientific Research Literature on Reading and Its Implications for Reading Instruction* (NIH Publication No. 00-4769). Washington, DC: U.S. Government Printing Office.

New York State Department of Education. 2011. *Race to the Top: "Bringing the Common Core to Life,"* Part 6. (Retrieved from http://usny.nysed.gov/rttt/resources/bringing-the-common-core-to-life.html.)

Nichols, S., and D. Berliner. 2007. *Collateral Damage: How High-Stakes Testing Corrupts America's Schools*. Cambridge, MA: Harvard University Press.

Obama, B. 2010. Address to National Governors Association. February 22. Accessed October 2, 2012. www.whitehouse.gov/photos-and-video/video/president-obama-calls-new-steps-prepare-children-college-and-careers#transcript.

Ohanian, S. 2012. "Here's How Bill Gates Gets the Common Core . . . or Something Called the Common Core." Accessed November 15, 2012. www.susanohanian.org/core.php?id=347.

Online Etymology Dictionary. Accessed January 7, 2013. www.etymonline.com/index.php?term=standard

Orellana, M. F. 2009. *Translating Childhoods: Immigrant Youth, Language, and Culture*. New Brunswick, NJ: Rutgers University Press.

Owocki, G. 2012. *The Common Core Lesson Book: Working with Increasingly Complex Literature, Informational Text, and Foundational Reading Skills*. Portsmouth, NH: Heinemann.

Payne, R. 2005. *A Framework for Understanding Poverty*. Baytown, TX: aha! Process, Inc.

Pearson, P. D. 2012. "Critical Issues Concerning the Common Core State Standards: Research, Policy, Practice." Paper presented at the annual meeting of the Literacy Research Association, San Diego, CA, November 30, 2012.

Perez-Pena. R. 2012a. "Waivers for 8 More States from No Child Left Behind." The *New York Times*, May 30, A13.

———. 2012b. "U.S. Bachelor Degree Rate Passes Milestone." The *New York Times,* February 23, 2012.

Porter-Magee, K. 2012. "Misdirection and Self-interest: How Heinemann and Lucy Calkins Are Re-Writing the Common Core." Accessed November 17, 2012. www .edexcellence.net/commentary/education-gadfly-daily/common-core-watch/2012 /misdirection-and-self-interest-how-Heinemann-and-Lucy-Calkins-are-rewriting-the -Common-Core.html.

Rainie, L., K. Zickuhr, K. Purcell, M. Madden, and J. Brenner. 2012. *The Rise of E-reading.* Washington, DC: Pew Internet and American Life Project. Accessed April 15, 2012. http://libraries.pewinternet.org/2012/04/04/the-rise-of-ereading.

Ravitch, D. 1995. *National Standards in American Education: A Citizen's Guide.* Washington, DC: Brookings Institute.

———. 2010. *The Death and the Life of the Great American School System: How Testing and Choice Are Undermining Education.* New York: Basic Books.

———. 2012. "Who Is David Coleman?" Accessed October 10, 2012. http:// dianeravitch.net/2012/05/19/who-is-david-coleman/.

Reardon, S. 2011. "The Widening Academic Achievement Gap Between the Rich and Poor: New Evidence and Possible Explanations." In *Whither Opportunity? Rising Inequality, Schools, and Children's Life Chances,* edited by G. Duncan and R. Murnane, 91–166. New York: Russell Sage Foundation.

Reardon, S., and K. Bischoff. 2011. "Income Inequality and Income Segregation." *American Journal of Sociology* 116: 1092–1153.

Reich, R. 2011. *Aftershock: The Next Economy and America's Future.* New York: Vintage.

Rosenblatt, L. (1978) 1994. *The Reader, the Text, the Poem: The Transactional Theory of the Literacy Work.* Carbondale, IL: Southern Illinois University.

Rotherham, D. 2011. "David Coleman: The Architect—School of Thought: 11 Education Activists for 2011." *Time.* Accessed October 10, 2012. www.time.com /time/specials/packages/article/0,28804,2040867_2040871_2040925,00.html.

Sahlberg, P. 2011. *Finnish Lessons.* New York: Teachers College.

Serafini, F. 2010. "Reading Multimodal Texts: Perceptual, Structural and Ideological Perspectives." *Children's Literature in Education* 41 (2): 85–104.

———. 2011. "Expanding Perspectives for Comprehending Visual Images in Multimodal Texts." *Journal of Adolescent and Adult Literacy* 54 (5): 342–50.

Shanahan, T., D. Fisher, and N. Frey. 2012. "The Challenge of Challenging Text." *Educational Leadership* 69 (6): 58–62. Accessed November 13, 2012. www.ascd .org/publications/educational-leadership/mar12/vol69/num06/The-Challenge-of -Challenging-Text.aspx.

Shannon, P. 2011. *Reading Wide Awake: Politics, Pedagogies, and Possibilities.* New York: Teachers College.

ShareMyLesson. 2012. "ShareMyLesson Website." Accessed November 15, 2012. www.sharemylesson.com.

Smith, A. 1776. *An Inquiry into the Nature and Causes of the Wealth of Nations.* Accessed October, 21, 2012. http://www2.hn.psu.edu/faculty/jmanis/adam-smith /Wealth-Nations.pdf.

Snowber, C. 2012. "Dance as a Way of Knowing." *New Directions for Adult and Continuing Education* 134: 53–60.

Sparks, S. D. 2012. "Experts Say Accountability Focus Stymies Assessment Research." *Education Week*, November 14, 7–9, 11.

Street, B. 2001. "The New Literacy Studies." In *Literacy: A Critical Sourcebook*, edited by E. Cushman, E. Kintgen, B. Kroll, and M. Rose, 430–42. Boston: Bedford/St. Martins.

Sullivan, P., and H. Tinberg, eds. 2006. *What Is College-Level Writing?* Urbana, IL: National Council of Teachers of English.

Toppo, G. 2012. "Common Core Standards Drive a Wedge in Education Circles." *USA Today*, April 28. Accessed October 21, 2012. http://usatoday30.usatoday.com/news /education/story/2012-04-28/common-core-education/54583192/1.

Tough, P. 2007. "The Class Consciousness Raiser." The *New York Times,* June 10. Accessed January 5, 2013. www.nytimes.com/2007/06/10/magazine/10payne-t .html?pagewanted=print&_r=0.

Trujillo, T., and M. Renee. 2012. *Pursuing Equity and Learning from Evidence,* October. National Education Policy Center. Accessed October 21, 2012. http:// nepc.colorado.edu/files/pb-turnaroundequity_0.pdf.

U.S. Bureau of Labor Statistics. 2012. "Employment Projections: Fastest Growing Occupations." Accessed October 14, 2012. www.bls.gov/emp/ep_table_103.htm.

U.S. Census Bureau. 2012. "The 2012 Statistical Abstract. Table 233 Educational Attainment by State: 1990 to 2009." Accessed October 14, 2012. http://www .census.gov/compendia/statab/cats/education/educational_attainment.html.

U.S. Census Bureau/The *New York Times*. 2012. "Income Stagnation and Inequality" [graphic]. The *New York* Times, October 23. Accessed October 23, 2012. www .nytimes.com/interactive/2012/10/24/us/politics/income-stagnation-and-inequality .html.

U.S. Education Delivery Institute. (2011). What we do. (Retrieved from www .deliveryinstitute.org/delivery-approach).

University of Maine: The Division of Student Affairs. 2012. "About Us." Accessed December 2, 2012. http://umaine.edu/studentaffairs/about-us/vision-and-mission/.

Vasquez, V., P. Albers. and J. C. Harste. 2010. From the personal to the worldwide web: Moving teachers into positions of critical interrogation. In B. Baker (Ed.). *The new literacies: Multiple perspectives on research and practice* (pp. 265–284). New York, NY: Guilford Press.

Vilhjalmsson, R., G. Kristjansdottir, and D. S. Ward. 2012. "Bodily Deviations and Body Image in Adolescence." *Youth & Society* 44 (3): 366–84.

Westendorf, E. 2012. "How to Use LearnZillion to Plan Common Core ELA Lessons." Accessed November 1, 2012. https://attendee.gotowebinar.com/recording/728197679 6401938688.

Whitehurst, G. 2009. *Don't Forget the Curriculum*. Washington, DC: Brookings Institute.

Williams, J., E. C. Homan, and S. Swoffard. 2011. *Supporting Students in a Time of Core Standards: English Language Arts: Grades 3–5*. Urbana, IL: National Council of Teachers of English.

Willinsky, J. 1990. *The New Literacy: Redefining Reading and Writing in the Schools*. New York: Routledge.

Willis, A. 2008. *Reading Comprehension Research and Testing in the U.S.: Undercurrents of Race, Class, and Power in the Struggle for Meaning*. New York: Lawrence Erlbaum Associates.

Wohlwend, K. 2011. *Playing Their Way into Literacies: Reading, Writing, and Belonging in the Early Childhood Classroom*. New York: Teachers College.

Wolf, A. 2002. *Does Education Matter?* New York: Penguin.

Wyckoff, E., and A. Doerman. 2007. *Annual Report to the Ohio Department of Education*. Dayton, OH: Dayton Academy.

Zollers, N., and K. Ramanathan. 1998. "For-Profit Charter Schools and Students with Disabilities: The Sordid Side of the Business of Schooling." *Phi Delta Kappan* 80 (4): 297–304.

# INDEX